Research About Nineteenth-Century Children and Books

A —ANNETTE A UN TRÈS JOLI PETIT AGNEAU.

MONOGRAPH NO. 17

Papers presented at a symposium held at the University of Illinois at Urbana-Champaign, April 27-28, 1979, and sponsored by the Graduate School of Library Science and the Committee on National Planning for Special Collections, Association for Library Service to Children, American Library Association.

"The Studio-Boy," St. Nicholas, 1892 (vol. 19, pt. 2), p. 647.

Research About Nineteenth-Century Children and Books
Portrait Studies

Edited by

SELMA K. RICHARDSON

University of Illinois
Graduate School of Library Science
Urbana-Champaign, Illinois

LIBRARY OF CONGRESS CATALOGING IN PUBLICATION DATA

Main entry under title:

Research about nineteenth-century children and books.

(Monograph - University of Illinois Graduate School of Library Science ; no. 17)
"A symposium held April 27 and 28, 1979, University of Illinois at Urbana-Champaign."
1. Children's literature--Congresses. I. Richardson, Selma K. II. Series: Illinois. University at Urbana-Champaign. Graduate School of Library Science. Monograph ; no. 17.
PN1009.A1R47   809'.89282   80-19165
ISBN 0-87845-055-6

B—BAPTISTE A UNE PAIRE DE GRANDES
BOTTES.

CONTENTS

C—CÉCILE EST CHARMÉE DE FAIRE ROULER
  SON CERCEAU.

D—DENIS PLEURE PARCEQU'IL A MAL AUX DENTS.

Introduction

The fourth symposium in a series about research in children's literature was held at the University of Illinois at Urbana-Champaign on April 27 and 28, 1979. The symposium was sponsored by the Committee on National Planning of Special Collections, Association for Library Service to Children, American Library Association, and the University of Illinois Graduate School of Library Science. Other symposia in the series have been Research, Social History and Children's Literature (Simmons College); Research, The Creative Process and Children's Literature (University of Washington); and Research in Folkloristic Materials for Children (University of North Carolina at Chapel Hill).

The symposium, "Portrait Studies: Research about Nineteenth-Century Children and Books," was designed to bring together portrait-ists, from novice to experienced, who are interested in depicting nineteenth-century children. A large gallery would not be required to exhibit the few research studies in history and literature which portray children of the 1800s or their books. There have been calls over the years for further studies; some findings have been reported in publications of several disciplines. This symposium was planned to provide a setting in which the problems and possibilities of creating nineteenth-century portraits—of studying children and books of the last century—could be explored. The people of several fields were invited to hear and discuss papers about nineteenth-century children and books.

The title for this symposium was decided upon to provide a focal point for the seemingly unwieldy but intricately related interests about children and literature. Researchers have dipped back as far as Roman times and have readily spanned, and even made linkages among, many centuries. In many ways, studies about the nineteenth century, and more so the twentieth, rely upon findings about earlier centuries. Studies of children, real and fictional, and studies of reading materials for children have engaged researchers in the fields of literature, history, art, education, religion, sociology, psychology, and library science. To provide a common meeting ground for social historians, literary critics, and bibliophiles, a title was chosen which would embrace their diverse and frequently specialized interests. Thus the title placed the emphasis upon the nineteenth century, but called together from many fields people interested in children and books. A number of participants commented that this was the first time to their knowledge that such a group had been assembled.

One other consideration that influenced the conceptualizing of the program should be mentioned. A pattern can be noted in some transatlantic crossings. Many of the books for children of the colonies and of the newly founded nation were brought from England. Before 1820 most books were Americanized by simply changing a few words. By the 1850s the United States was furnishing reading material for English children. Today there are English and American authors producing for both countries. With regard to research studies, the pattern is not so advanced. The comprehensive and scholarly work of Darton and the books by Avery about the nineteenth century must be consulted due to the lack of their counterparts in the United States. Thus it seemed appropriate to summon Avery to the symposium that we might learn from her efforts and be inspired to hasten the appearance of studies comparable to the models England has furnished.

Early in the planning stages, specific purposes were stated which the symposium was to serve. Among these early statements were several which the participants in their evaluations of the symposium indicated had been more than satisfactorily met:

Draw together people representing many fields of study who share a common interest in the subject of the symposium;

Present speakers knowledgeable about some facets of the subject;
Allow for exchange of ideas, information, opinions, and findings about
nineteenth-century children and books;
Identify research collections of historical children's materials;
Encourage further studies about nineteenth-century children and books.

This very list suggests that a publication presenting the speeches that were given can reflect but a portion of the events of the symposium. Nevertheless, the speeches represent the part of the proceedings that can be cast in a book format. This publication has been prepared in response to the many requests to publish the proceedings from those who attended the symposium as well as from many who were unable to attend. Comments made during the discussion periods following each speech have not been included in this book.

Gillian Avery, well known for her *Nineteenth Century Children* and *Childhood's Pattern*, came from Oxford to fill the role of keynote speaker. In her first speech she described how her interest in nineteenth-century children's books evolved and her use of the resources of the Bodleian. In her second presentation Avery discussed the treatment of children's books as social history.

Walter L. Arnstein evaluated research studies of childhood from a historian's point of view. His overview and critical assessments of the body of research provide a framework and basis for understanding, which would undoubtedly be essential to anyone planning to investigate reading materials for children of earlier centuries. His annotated bibliography should serve as a useful guide.

There are many research collections of children's materials of the nineteenth century; descriptions of any one of them would have been pertinent to the symposium. It was decided, however, to highlight one which might not be very well known. Margaret N. Coughlan comments upon the holdings of American children's books and other materials at Winterthur Museum in Delaware. For those seeking further descriptions of the study and collecting of historical children's books in the United States, the issue of *Library Trends** that appeared at the time of the symposium will be helpful.

While the emphasis of Friday's speakers was upon the English scene and the implements of researchers, Saturday's speakers reported research studies about American children's books. The diversity of approaches to the study of children's reading matter is well represented in the four reports. Karcher was led to Lydia Maria Child through her interest in

*Richardson, Selma K., ed. "The Study and Collecting of Historical Children's Books," *Library Trends*, vol. 27, no. 4, Spring 1979.

social history. As a part of her study, Karcher investigated the *Juvenile Miscellany* edited by Child. Koppes employed techniques of literary criticism to analyze selected works for children by Burnett and Twain. A bio-bibliographic study of Sophie May was discussed by Doll. Christy's report, illustrated by slides, dealt with the first appearances of stories in children's periodicals of the nineteenth century. Since many of the works mentioned are known to today's readers, the final presentation not only effectively reviewed the output of the century, but served as a reminder that some of the works for the present generation of children have celebrated or soon will be celebrating their centenaries.

The four reports about American children's books helped to underline another feature of this symposium: all were made by "new" researchers. Bixler did her study for her doctoral dissertation; the other three reports were based on graduate studies. This new blood should surely strengthen our hopes for a substantial body of research about early children's books in the United States.

John Mackay Shaw, luncheon speaker, captivated the audience with his thoughts and remarks about poetry for children. The written format cannot do justice to the warmth and humaneness Shaw exudes. Some measure of the sureness and conviction with which he spoke can, however, be caught in his forthright statements. His talk, too, aptly linked the nineteenth and twentieth centuries, from his opening comment that he was born in the century under discussion to his closing challenge to bring our children the fine poetry written years ago. Shaw has given his collection of books to Florida State University, but continues to add to *Childhood in Poetry*, the ten-volume index to the collection published by Gale Research Company.

Two sessions of the symposium cannot be adequately reported in the published proceedings. On Friday evening the participants met in small groups constructed around topics in which interest had been expressed on the registration form. The chair of each group briefly summarized his/her findings to launch the discussion. The areas of interest and the persons leading the groups are listed below:

The Alcott Family
　　Bruce A. Ronda, Assistant Professor, Skidmore College
Changing Moral Values in Children's Books of the Nineteenth Century
　　Christa Kamenetsky, Associate Professor, Central Michigan University
Childhood Spirituality among Romantic Writers
　　Robert L. Platzner, Chair, Department of Humanities, California State University, Sacramento

Nineteenth-Century Fantasy for Children
     Anita Moss, Instructor, University of North Carolina at Charlotte
Nineteenth-Century Magazines for Children
     Mary June Roggenbuck, Associate Professor, Catholic University of
     America
Research Collections of Children's Books
     Barbara Maxwell, Librarian, Free Library of Philadelphia
Writing Stories with Nineteenth-Century Settings for Children Today
     Avi Wortis, Librarian, Trenton State College

Late Friday afternoon the participants went to the Rare Book Room of the University Library to view an exhibit of early children's books prepared by graduate students enrolled in History of Children's Literature, a course offered by the Graduate School of Library Science. This is the fourth consecutive year that an exhibit has been presented by the students. The preparation of the exhibit is used as an instructional device to help students in a survey course identify some themes which they can pursue, to give them an opportunity to probe the collections of the university, and to provide them with experience in packaging ideas for consumption by both casual and astute viewers. The title of the 1979 exhibit was "ABC, About Books for Children: To Instruct and to Amuse." Each student prepared several cases for the subject she had selected. The sections of the exhibit and their architects are listed below in the recommended sequence for viewing.

ABCs from Adamant Instruction to Zany Amusement
     Paula Sieben
A Literature for Children
     Jackie Ziff
Maria Edgeworth
     Ann West
Books for Victorian Boys and Girls
     Joyce Martin
Thomas Bewick
     Dale Bourassa
The Tales of Peter Parley
     Cynthia Helms
A History of Sir Thomas Thumbe
     Joanne Kelly

The involvement of students here and elsewhere in the program bodes well for the future of the study of the history of children's books.
     The sessions of the symposium were capably chaired by people associated with the University of Illinois: Alice Lohrer, Professor

Emerita; Dorothy Matthews, Associate Professor of English; N. Frederick Nash, Rare Book Librarian; and Ina Robertson and Agnes Stahlschmidt, doctoral students.

Gale Research Company subsidized some of the expenses of Mr. Shaw.

The registrants indicated that they were exceedingly well pleased by the symposium. Some of the items from the forms used to evaluate the symposium might serve, for those unable to attend, to relay the ambience that the printed proceedings cannot convey. The participants gave strong support to the following statements:

The symposium was a high-quality experience.
The symposium was intellectually stimulating.
The symposium experience provided valuable information.
Research collections heretofore unknown were discussed.
Opportunities were provided for interactions with speakers.
A superior trait of the symposium was the chance to interact with colleagues.
People were identified with whom information and findings will probably be exchanged.
The symposia series should be continued.

SELMA K. RICHARDSON

E —ÉDOUARD VA GAIEMENT À L'ÉCOLE, AVEC SES LIVRES.

F—FANCHON FAIT UNE CRAVATE POUR SON FRÈRE.

The Researcher's Craft:
Designs and Implements

GILLIAN AVERY

A small girl wrote to me recently saying, "I enjoy reading your books very much. I hope to be a writter when I grow up so can you give me any tips also how many degrees do you have to take to write."

Even so recently as twenty years ago, she probably would not have put in that question about the degrees—for in England, at any rate, the feeling that a university education provides the key to all future achievement is comparatively recent. I was obliged to write back and admit that I had no degrees, and I must at the outset of this paper make it perfectly clear to you here that I am wholly uneducated, and that I am amazed at my audacity in presuming to address you about techniques of research when my own researches have pursued such an unprofessional and idiosyncratic course. Of course, many people without any formal direction have contrived to turn themselves into meticulous and learned

7

scholars, but though there were moments—now long ago—when I hoped that this could happen to me, that I might perhaps become another Harvey Darton, I have now accepted that I shall never be anything more than a muddled amateur.

My fondness for old children's books began when I was eight or nine and was given Louey Chisholm and Amy Steadman's *A Staircase of Stories*, consisting, as the title suggests, of stories graded in difficulty, beginning with exercises in cumulative repetition like "The Old Woman and Her Pig," and finishing with Daudet's "The Last Class," which, though the style is deceptively simple, demands an almost adult response. The Misses Chisholm and Steadman had no inhibitions whatever about retelling stories and omitting elements that were not to their liking, and they had included several chapters from Mrs. Sherwood's *The History of the Fairchild Family*. This had been originally published in three parts between 1818 and 1847, and is perhaps the book most universally known to the Victorian young. Even in the Edwardian period it was so famous that a society hostess gave a party to which everybody was bidden to appear dressed as a character from *The Fairchild Family*; but by the 1930s (when I assume *A Staircase of Stories* was published; it is undated) it was wholly unread, so that the editors could remove all the Calvinistic religious teaching—all the sermons and prayers, Mr. Fairchild's identification of himself as a surrogate for God on earth, the floggings, the visits to deathbeds and the gallows, the children's examination of their consciences, their assessment of the state of grace of others, the constant reiteration of the terrible depravity of man's nature—and leave a wholly delightful picture of gentle domesticity, where the children eat hot buttered toast, play with their pet hare and their magpie, fall out of the swing in the barn, are a little naughty but not much, and are soon enfolded in the arms of loving parents.

"During its vogue," Harvey Darton wrote of *The Fairchild Family*, "and after, it was perhaps as widely read, as completely ridiculed, and as honestly condemned by child-lovers, as any English book ever written for children. It has deserved all three fates. It contains in its mass of minatory and exegetic detail two features not surpassed elsewhere. The prose Mrs. Sherwood wielded was masterly; and no one ever described very simple childish pleasures—especially those of the table—with more obvious enjoyment in them. The meals eaten by the little Fairchilds, even if they teach lessons about greed, make the mouth water to this day. The buttered toast...alas, so prodigally wasted."[1]

The editors of *A Staircase of Stories* recognized these qualities too, and (as I am sure Mrs. Sherwood would have said) they winnowed the chaff from the grain—and threw away the grain. The unscrupulous scouring of the original text did undoubtedly produce excellent stories, and it was done so skillfully that even reading it with adult eyes it is impossible to detect the omissions and where the seams occur unless one knows the original intimately. In the modern climate of responsibility toward the true text—at least so far as the serious publishers are concerned—no conscientious editor would dare emasculate a work in this way. But in the 1930s they were delightfully carefree. All the same, when I am tempted to disapprove of this sort of tampering, I have to remember how much pleasure the revised *Fairchild* stories, and such retellings as my much-loved *Child Stories from Dickens*, gave me.

Then, when I was a young person of fourteen—by which time World War II had begun—a family uprooted from their own home asked us to house a few of their books. Among them was a big omnibus volume of old children's stories reprinted from the original texts. In this I found Juliana Horatia Ewing's delightful evocation of the sort of childhood that had vanished even by her time: *A Flat Iron for a Farthing*. It was the first book that I really recognized as being "old"—such books as *Little Women*, *Katy*, and even *The Fairchild Family* had seemed timeless, and one read them without consciously clothing the characters in old-fashioned dress. After that I did in a desultory way look out for old children's books in the secondhand bookshops of the small town where I lived (there were four or five thriving ones then, all vanished now). And when at the age of nineteen I began working in London, I used to spend most of my lunch hour pottering in and out of the many secondhand bookshops in the Charing Cross Road area. I could only afford to spend a shilling or two; my salary in those days was four pounds a week, of which a large proportion went to my railway season ticket to and from my parents' home in Surrey. Plenty of people might nevertheless have thereby acquired treasures, but I hasten to say that this never happened to me. It would never happen to one of the Averys, who have a strong family propensity to bark up the wrong tree. I often thought I had discovered unique and valuable editions, and tried to interest such firms as Maggs Brothers and Quaritch in them; there would be a blissful period of two or three days while I waited for their reply to my letter, during which I would mentally spend the fortune that I anticipated (on an odd volume from an early nineteenth-century edition of Pope, for instance). But after a while even I grew pessimistic. Most often my purchases would land me (in a typically Avery way) with volume two of a novel from which volume one had long decades ago been detached.

But I did read most of the books that I bought (I remember even reading two volumes of Whiffen's very lame translation of Tasso's *Jerusalem Delivered*, though that was so I could boast about it to my American penfriend), and in that way became an admirer of Mrs. Ewing. So when in the late 1950s Robin Denniston moved from the children's book department of Collins (who had published my first children's book in 1957) and established himself at Faith Press (a small Anglican publishing concern which he had ambitions, I think, of turning into a big general publisher), and asked whether I could suggest any out-of-copyright children's books that might be worth reprinting, I could name several. There were my favorite Mrs. Ewings. There was also *Father Phim* by Annie Keary, a delightful and unusually sympathetic account of troubled nineteenth-century Ireland. It was probably written in 1856 but first published in 1879, a time when the vast majority of Protestant books for children still made a point of lambasting the crude and wicked beliefs of the Roman Catholic church, and stressing that the only good Catholics were the ones who saw the errors of their ways and were converted to Protestantism. *Father Phim* presents the Irish with warm understanding. Annie Keary puts forward the point of view of both parties—the English landlords, who were struggling to farm their land well and make a living out of it but fighting a losing battle against the lackadaisical, good-tempered idleness of the tenants; and the tenants themselves, who saw this as an attempt by the English to grind even more and more money out of them and keep them in abject poverty. It is, in my experience, almost unique in Victorian children's fiction in England because of its breadth of tolerance. There is not the slightest sign that Annie Keary felt there was any difference between her heroine, the daughter of an Anglican clergyman, and the Irish peasants on her grandfather's estate—and this at a time when rigid class and religious barriers were implicit in the stories of her contemporaries.

I found *Father Phim* in the Hampstead Subscription Library, a decaying private lending library near my parents-in-law's home in north London. I had been given an introduction to the librarian, whom I remember as an elderly lady who seemed to be doing the job voluntarily, and to be at her wits' end to know how to cope with a mass of books which belonged to the taste of a long-vanished generation, and which nobody wanted to borrow. She was delighted that I showed an interest in the children's section, and was almost deliriously eager for me to buy them and get them out of her way; she didn't want more than a few shillings apiece, and didn't think they were really worth that. I had an uneasy feeling, which I pushed to the back of my mind, that the trustees of the library might take a very different view, but I hastily carried off most of her Victorian children's novels, and took them back to Manchester where my husband was then teaching.

That coup provided the foundation of my collection. But I would have probably added to it much more gradually if I had not been asked sometime in the 1960s to write a book about children's books—I suppose on the strength of the introductions I had written to Faith Press's reprints. At that time—though this now seems incredible in the light of the almost obsessive interest taken in children's books—there were only four works which dealt with them historically. Towering above the other three was, of course, Harvey Darton's *Children's Books in England* (which also deals with American ones), subtitled *Five Centuries of Social Life*. This had first been published in 1932 and was reissued in 1958. It is a giant of a book approaching the subject with a majestic breadth of learning, a sense of proportion, a lightness of touch, that has never been subsequently equalled, and beside which most other studies of the subject seem fussy and parochial, nearly always so obsessed with particular trees that they are incapable of taking in the landscape. There were also Percy Muir's *English Children's Books 1600-1900*, published in 1954, mostly with the bibliographer and collector in mind; and *A Critical History of Children's Literature* by Cornelia Meigs and others (1953), which was written from the point of view of the librarian and teacher. *Tellers of Tales* by Roger Lancelyn Green had been originally written for children and then upgraded for adults in 1953, and deals with the subject biographically, as the title suggests.

It was Harvey Darton's conception of the child's book as an aspect of social life that shaped my own approach, even though at first I found his own book tantalizing and puzzling in the immensity of its range. Only with the penultimate chapter, "The Sixties: Alice and After," did I begin to feel the ground was at all familiar. In all the preceding chapters he had dwelt on writers whom I had rarely heard of and certainly never read, books that were not to be seen outside the great national libraries or very specialized collections. I knew, however, that he must be my guide, and recklessly I stepped out behind him. I wanted to approach the history of children's books not from the literary point of view, but as part of social history. I wanted to give some account of the changing ideals of child behavior as depicted in the books that adults purveyed for the consumption of the young.

And then, of course, the problem arose of how I was to lay hands on these books. We had been living in Manchester since 1954; there was a good public library and a university library, but neither of these, of course, contained historical children's books. There was, and still is, an important collection in the public library in Preston, Lancashire, some two hours' journey away, but with a small child it would have been impossible for me to spend anything more than the odd day there. But I was undaunted and determined, and I decided to try to buy the books. I put an advertisement in the personals column of the *Times*. As far as I remember it just said boldly that an author wished to buy Victorian children's books. In 1963 these were still available at a moderate price so it did not seem, as it would today, a millionaire's approach. The response was amazing. There were, it seemed, scores of old ladies who wanted a kind home for much-loved family books, and they sent me lists of titles beside which I scribbled the price I was prepared to give—I don't think it was ever more than a few shillings. And then within a few days the parcels would arrive bulgy and bursting, tied up by trembling old fingers. I made it a point of honor that none of the books so received would ever be sold in my lifetime.

Mostly the books were not very valuable; they were storybooks of the 1860s onward, many in bad condition by the time I got them; but they provided what I wanted—a generous sample of what Victorian youth had read. I didn't care if the authors were unknown to me, it was the epoch that mattered and the mood of the times. One or two people said that they had earlier books, did it matter that they weren't Victorian? I think I added on an extra shilling or two for those. And there was one lady, with the memorable name of Ernestine Lady Dobbs, who lived in a house with the even more memorable name of Samphire, somewhere in Ireland, with whom I carried on a long and tantalizing correspondence. All her children's books, she said, dated from before 1820, did I mind? No, I said vehemently and by return post, I certainly did not mind. Then, she wrote back, she would make a point of going down into the library and looking them out. I pictured a huge eighteenth-century pile, damply decaying under weeping Irish skies, falling to pieces around her. But if they were before 1800, would I mind that? Or perhaps they were too early for me? Of course that was all right, I said magnanimously. Then she would see what she could do; any day now she would have a look in the library. But she never did, or rather her counselors stepped in my way, and she wrote a sad letter saying that her trustees had forbidden her to part with any of her books, though she had so much wanted me to have them.

So I had to do without the Samphire collection, and depended for the chapter on the Georgian books largely upon my collaborator, Angela Bull, who was then doing a research degree at Oxford, and was in any case going to write two chapters on fairy tales. From Harvey Darton I sifted the names that I wanted. I began with his chapters on the theorists, Thomas Day and the Edgeworths and French influence. I had managed to buy *Sandford and Merton* and the *Parent's Assistant* and *Practical Education*, so I could cope with those, and also with Mrs. Barbauld, and Mrs.

Trimmer's *History of the Robins.* (I must here praise Garland Press's enterprise in issuing, from New York, all these seminal works essential to the study of the history of children's books, but otherwise unavailable outside the great national primary collections.) Angela Bull read and made elaborate notes upon such writers as Mary Belson Elliot, Arabella Argus, Priscilla Wakefield, and the Kilner sisters, whose names I had found in Harvey Darton's chapters on the moral tale. And such of their writings as looked especially rewarding I managed to read for myself in brief visits to the British Museum or the the Bodleian Library in Oxford.

The later books I had by now mostly managed to acquire for myself. I was not attempting to cover the whole of the nineteenth-century output—not that anybody could; I wanted to take random samplings. The publishers' advertisements at the back of books were a great help; they suggested the names of authors popular and prolific in their own time, though by now wholly forgotten, and some of them I investigated in the British Museum or at Oxford. The names Esme Stuart, Annette Lyster, Emma Leslie and Emma Marshall occur to me now—ladies who did very well out of the demand then for Sunday school prizes, which was the main motivating force for the children's book trade in the late Victorian period. A book that I found of immense value was a little work, hardly more than a pamphlet, published for teachers and those with the responsibility of providing books for prizes and for parish libraries: Charlotte Yonge's *What Books to Give and What to Lend,* published in 1887. Miss Yonge had appended comments under her suggestions, which had their own period flavor. She remarked, of course, on the moral teaching that the books provided (this factor was paramount), but also added whether the stories had pleased the classes to whom she had read them.

So out of this fitful and amateurish research I produced *Nineteenth Century Children: Heroes and Heroines in English Children's Stories, 1780-1900.*[2] As soon as it was in print (in 1965), I knew how bad it was. I can only feebly excuse myself by repeating that there then was very little written on the subject from which I could have corrected my errors. I had never managed to lay my hands on a copy of Judith St. John's catalog of the Osborne Collection, for instance, which had been published in Toronto in 1958; now I would find it impossible to work without it. And apart from Angela Bull, I then knew nobody who was working in the same field. Roger Lancelyn Green, for instance, who has more facts at his fingertips about biographical and bibliographical points than anyone living, would have saved me from many mistakes. Angela herself had had great difficulty in finding a supervisor at Oxford for her thesis on fantasy and fairy tales. Eventually she was assigned to Lord David Cecil (I

suppose because it was felt he understood the Victorian novel), but he had to draw all his knowledge of the subject from what his daughter read in the nursery.

Not only was I inaccurate, I was also unfair in some of my judgments, particularly of the evangelical writers. A copy of Paul Sangster's admirable study of early evangelical education, *Pity My Simplicity* (Epworth Press, 1963), was put into my hands when I was correcting my own page proofs. In agony I tried to rewrite bits of my text—which of course was both ineffectual and expensive. As soon as the book was published I wanted to write something better, something that would correct mistakes and cover ground that I realized I had left wholly unexplored. When I approached the publishers in the 1970s, they put two alternatives before me: I could either make a few alterations for a new edition of *Nineteenth Century Children*, or write a new book. I chose to do the latter.

This time it was much easier. We were now living in Oxford and I could spend all the time I wanted in the Bodleian. And the John Johnson Collection of Ephemeral Printing had moved from the premises of the Oxford University Press where I had first encountered it in 1950, and was housed in the New Library at the Bodleian.

The John Johnson collection has been the scene of nearly all my research in the last few years, and I realize to my astonishment that probably now I know it better than almost anybody else; certainly I have known it longer. It is difficult to convey an adequate idea of its scope. John Johnson had the idea that the history of a people is written in its toffee papers and toothpaste tubes, and he set out to collect all that and a great deal more. All sorts of things that are usually the subject of separate collections form just a tiny part of this one—postage stamps, for instance, matchbox tops, Christmas cards, children's books, visiting cards. There are about twenty boxes of menus, twenty more of school prospectuses, boxes of copybooks, the papers that wrap oranges, each beautifully mounted on a card sheet. There are shop catalogs, cigar bands, political posters, railway timetables, tram tickets, a huge section on typography and the history of printing; Victorian pornography, comics, theater programs, manuals on agriculture and firearms, notices of executions or auctions, ballads and broadsheets, tracts, dog licenses, board games, theater tickets. And though Johnson himself made the outbreak of war, 1939, the *terminus ante quem* (he said that wartime air raid precautions ephemera alone would fill room space many times the whole existing space of the collection), it is still being added to. While working there I have seen people bringing in yogurt pots, undergraduate magazines, political handouts. But to all this mass of material there is no catalog, nor can there ever be one. All there is is a list of the titles of the boxes and folders, and their shelf numbers.

My acquaintance with the collection began in the 1950s when I was working as a junior illustrations editor at the University Press. John Johnson, though he had retired from his position of Printer to the University in 1946, still kept his collection on the Press premises in Walton Street—those handsome neoclassical buildings standing round a pleasant quadrangle that must be taken by many visitors to Oxford as a college. My work as illustrations editor involved finding material to illustrate the *Oxford Junior Encyclopaedia* which the Press was then in the process of publishing, volume by volume, and from time to time I would be dispatched to ask Dr. Johnson if he could supply subjects from his collection. The excitement of these trips was considerable. For one thing, it meant treading over the boundaries of the publishing side into the printing side with its heady, hot smell of printer's ink, and the sound of machines thundering away below. (The Oxford University Press and possibly the one at Cambridge must be among the very few houses where printers and publishers work in the same premises—though that, in my time, did not mean that one was allowed to have any contact with the printing staff. Quite the reverse; there was a special intermediary who negotiated on our behalf, a thoroughly frustrating business.) I would knock at the door which was labeled Constance Meade Collection—to the end, John Johnson insisted on paying elaborate deference to this benefactor—and then there I was, in the presence.

Dr. Johnson—he had been given an honorary degree by his university, and unlike most of those honored in this way, chose to be called by it—would be found poised on a high stool like some captive eagle, scanning the contents of one of his box files. He was a huge, bony man, with a craggy face and iron gray hair—one of the most terrifying men I had ever met. Or rather, though his manner was one of old-fashioned courtesy toward women (and there was always a devoted female attendant hovering in the shadows), I was aware of his capacity to terrify. His family life was, I gathered, stormy; people spoke with awe of the crockery that hurtled through the air in the Johnson home in Headington. As Printer he had been an autocrat; with dogged and grim determination he had worked in 1925 to turn the University Press into a modern printing establishment—and many battles had to be fought to achieve that. When he first went to Walton Street during World War I, he had daily worked from 4 a.m. until late at night. During the Second World War, he had lived and slept on the premises. And though there were tantalizing piles of fascinating objects scattered round him—Victorian toys and games and valentines were the ones I particularly remember—I never dared to ask to be allowed to handle them, never ventured even to be caught with my head turned in their direction. I would ask for the subject we wanted to illustrate (an old tram ticket, perhaps, or a political poster of the last century); arrangement would be made for it to be photographed, and I would go.

John Johnson had been inspired to form this collection of ephemera by his excavations in Egypt before World War I, which was where he had his first experience of administration. "More than forty years ago," he wrote to a friend eighteen months before he died, "I was spending my winters with large gangs of *fellahin* digging the rubbish-mounds of Graeco-Roman cities in Egypt for the written materials—the wastepaper—of those ages....Often I used to look over those dark and crumbling sites and wonder what could be done to treat the background of our own English civilization with the same minute care with which we scholars were treating the ancient."

The collecting had begun as soon as he joined the Press—at first, it seemed, with the idea of book illustration:

> Every evening as I went home from work I remarked the queues outside the cinemas and made up my mind that the art of illustration of books, particularly perhaps of school books, but also of all books, could be made to satisfy the same instinct in mankind. I set to work, timidly at first, but soon with more confidence, on what appeared to be the miscellany of the world, to show what was really the order and development of it. Trivial things like the development of advertisements on our hoardings, the many-sided interests of postage stamps, the development of the journals, all the ephemera of our lives, were brought into the compass of illustration; and I venture to think that the more ordinary they were, the more compelling they were in their new alignment. Soon a school history, illustrated in this way, caught the imagination of the market and was selling in all its forms something like 40,000 copies a year.
>
> Collections came into being, photographic and of scraps, all designed to illustrate books....At that time in my house let me confess that there was the growing material of illustration for a different book under each bed, a primitive and not unsatisfactory dodge for keeping the material apart.

There were others with the same idea (Johnson named six of them), all of them with this same jackdaw instinct:

> All of them started in their own way collecting. I remember my old friend Sir Emery Walker telling me that he used to keep an old commode in his room with its lifting lid, which was known as "Proctor's rubbish box." Day by day all the common discarded papers of life were dropped into the pan of the commode and later went on to Proctor. Proctor kept every railway ticket that he did not give up, and he did not give up a great many, every bus ticket of his daily rounds, every receipt,

every paper bag. Only one of the six men lived to sort his material. And by a series of accidents some of the material of all six men came to us.

Of his own collection, Johnson wrote:

> It is difficult to describe it except by saying that it is everything which would ordinarily go into the wastepaper basket after use, everything printed which is not actually a book. Another way of describing it is to say that we gather everything which a museum or library would not ordinarily accept if it were offered as a gift; so that these university collections fill a gap in the world which nothing else really fills....I think I can say that the width of these collections as they stand, has no other counterpart in the world. Collected on this wide area they render us open to the banter of the world....
>
> Already there must be a thousand boxes or cloth folders, housing a million and more examples of the ephemera of our lives; they vary as widely as such minutiae as bus tickets, calling cards, or cigar bands on the one hand, and magnificent broadsides or cartoons on the other. On the social side all forms of transport are there, and on the socio-political side there is...even the debris of the women's suffrage movement,...the propaganda of the streets, and the later litter of the Communist and Fascist movements.
>
> I challenge...any to suggest any subject in which we can record no evidence at all! Yes, there is the birth of the football pool there, and all kinds of bookies' tickets and wireless licences.

The collection also benefited from the Bodleian's crisis of space in the 1930s. The New Library had not yet been built and the copyright intake was increasing yearly. And those in charge felt a strong aversion to the ephemera which the library had been obliged to house: the booksellers' catalogs, for instance, calendars, illuminated texts, advertisements. There was a subsequent purge, and many of the eliminated items found their way to Johnson's "Sanctuary of Printing," as he styled it, and can be seen there now, with the canceled Bodleian stamp on them.

By the time I encountered Dr. Johnson, the collection occupied more than 2,500 folio filing boxes, several hundred large folders, several cabinets of drawers, and many hundreds of volumes. They were ranged on shelves in four communicating rooms (known as "cabins"), and Dr. Johnson appeared to know every item in them; he was never in my memory at a loss to know where to lay his hands upon an item that was wanted. We saw each other rather often. In the end he became quite fond of me—as he had been of every other young woman whom he had encountered (it was men whom he disliked), and he even said that he would present me with a key to the collection so that I could use it at my will. (I remember the fleeting look of amusement on the face of the attendant nymph as he said this.) I left Oxford in 1954—without the key, it need not be said.

I had to wait until the 1970s, by which time we were back in Oxford, before I was able to investigate the collection freely. When Dr. Johnson had died in 1956, the University Press had been perplexed to know what they should do about the administration of the collection. In the end they recalled Lilian Thrussell to look after it. She was a most remarkable woman. She had, I gathered, once been the domestic help of the Johnson household, but had been taken over by Dr. Johnson. It was she who must largely have been responsible for the beautiful mounting of the smaller items, the labeling and organization of the files. But much more than that, a great deal of the collecting and selection had been left to her. When the collection was transferred to the Bodleian in 1968, she went with it and became one of the library staff. She was still there when I rediscovered the collection, and was an enormous asset, as her memory was as good as Dr. Johnson's. I could ask for some subject that I once remembered, vaguely, having seen—"A picture of a Victorian scullery with a maid wearing pattens, Lil. Can you place it?" And she'd reply, "An advertisement for washing soda. You'll find it in the first box of Soaps."

It was, I may say, extraordinary to handle the boxes and folders for myself. In the past no outsider had ever been allowed to. Dr. Johnson, or possibly one of his attendants, had found what one asked for. Now one was free to rummage at will, to climb up the ladders and pull down box after box. But Lil was losing her old attack. I don't think she ever really cared for being on the staff of the library. She came in less and less often, and then she ceased to come at all, leaving, as I remember, a pair of shoes and a shopping bag as a mute suggestion that perhaps one day she might feel disposed to return. Without her it must be very difficult for any stranger to use the resources of the collection properly, for there is no full-time curator, and the young assistants who are appointed to help with it are usually interested in only one small area, and tend to leave after about a year. When I called there to gather materials for this paper, I found that the two people who had been dealing with John Johnson matters—the staffing quota is officially 1.5 persons—had both left. Staffing will always be a problem. The collection is housed in three high-ceilinged, communicating rooms (three cabins, as against Dr. Johnson's original four), and though a highly intelligent librarian is required, a lot of the work is undoubtedly tedious, a filing clerk's job, and calls for muscle and a good head for heights, as one clambers up the terrifying ladders to pull out the heavy box files about twenty feet above the floor. And it will never be used by very many people (which is probably as well, as so many of the items are very frail), as it takes years to learn the scope of the collection, and only a very few are now allowed loose in it to rummage for themselves.

When I came to write *Childhood's Pattern*, I found that the collection contained a large number of children's books. The obscure and trite was just as good for my purpose as the well-written, better-known story, and there in the boxes were a considerable number of early examples arranged in chronological order. There were also a fair number of comics, but no more than one or two samples of a given title, which made my work infinitely easier than if I had had to wade through the national collection of newsprint at Colindale.

But though I drew upon the Johnson collection for books in this instance, it is for picture research that it is so invaluable, and as this is the only sort of research at which I am at all skilled, I perhaps ought to give some account of my experience. Picture research is now an industry, and with every year there seem fewer words in a book and more illustrations, but when I started the term had not, I think, been invented. It was my job on the *Oxford Junior Encyclopaedia*, but they called me an "illustrations editor." We would get the text of the articles in the volume we were currently working on (the volumes went by subjects), and my senior would make a list of the illustrations she suggested, and I then had to find them. There are, of course, agencies who at the drop of a hat will send you a vast selection of pictures on any subject you care to name, but we avoided them if at all possible, because they were so accessible to everybody. I still can instantly recognize if a book has been illustrated from agency sources—the pictures tend to be depressingly familar, and lack the element of idiosyncratic choice. But to pursue one's own line was often frustrating and infuriating. I might have seen the perfect portrait of Warren Hastings, say, reproduced in some biography. It is useless to ask publishers to provide original material they have reproduced in one of their books. They have either lost it or won't part with it; I soon learned not to ask. They may divulge what their source was, but they usually don't bother to reply, or they have forgotten, or destroyed all their records. But this particular portrait of Warren Hastings I did manage to trace back to a public building in Calcutta. There was then the problem of getting it photographed, of finding an Indian firm who would do it, of keeping them up to the mark, urging them to do it in time, pleading with them not to let me down. I got that particular picture, but I was not always successful, and I couldn't always wait. There was one item, I remember, a picture belonging to a Rothschild, that could not be photographed until all the European Rothschilds had met in solemn conclave—Count Edouard, Count Leopold and the rest—and given their consent. I had to give that one up.

But to do picture research for my own books was delightful. I had only myself to please, and if I found some subject tricky I would give it up; there was no implacable senior to urge me to make greater efforts. And nearly all of it could be done from the Bodleian and the Johnson collection.

Illustrating *Childhood's Pattern* was straightforward; I used my own books or the library's books. I had made notes of what I wanted as I wrote the text. More challenging were the illustrations to a book that I wrote in 1974, which I called *The Echoing Green*. This was a collection of memories of childhood in the nineteenth century. There was a child who remembered how the news of the battle of Trafalgar was brought by the mail coach to the small Midland town where she lived; a twelve-year old who had been a boy soldier during the Napoleonic wars; another who had been a railway navvy; a foundling who had emigrated to Canada; an English Quaker family who had settled in Ohio; a boy who remembered the first railway coming to his town, and so on to the end of the century, when a child remembered the Diamond Jubilee of Queen Victoria and a young chorister described how he had sung at her funeral. The idea was to span the century, through childish memories, and I set them in the framework of Mary Howitt's memoirs. She was the little girl who could remember the battle of Trafalgar, and her life included two Golden Jubilees, of George III and Queen Victoria, and vast change.

I have never enjoyed writing a book more, and I became so attached to the children that I hated finishing it. To choose the autobiographical material was not difficult; I had been collecting it for some time with this in view, and a lot of the books we possessed ourselves. Those that we did not I borrowed from the London Library. This wonderful institution is a godsend to all authors. It is a huge private library in St. James's Square with the grave, friendly atmosphere of a London club. They buy every serious book that is published in England, and a good many foreign ones, and a fair proportion of fiction. They were established in the middle of the last century, so that they have most of the Victorian books that one wants. One can go and look out the books for oneself, or country members can ask for them to be sent. The subscription when I joined was £20; it is now probably £30 annually. But my husband invested a small legacy in a life subscription, so that the library is now at our disposal in perpetuity.

The illustrations required more work—and it was to the Johnson collection that I turned, rummaging haphazardly in likely folders. There was a convenient one labeled just "The Social Day," and here desperate assistants seemed to have tossed items that couldn't be placed anywhere else. There I found an exquisite drawing, unsigned, of a Regency ball that perfectly illustrated the description one of my writers had given of fashionable life in Edinburgh in 1815. An engraving of about the same date, showing a family clustered round their mother in the drawing room, a harp in the background, seemed to have been specially drawn for the text. And, of course, I could always tamper with my text to fit the picture—in a perfectly honorable way. I found a delightful drawing of a young woman spinning. I remembered how Mary Howitt had described seeing her mother spin, so I inserted this into my text. I was looking through the *Illustrated London News* for a particular year, and saw a vivid picture of a railway accident, engine lying on its side, wreckage strewn everywhere. One of my writers had been in this very train, his brother had run down the line to fetch help, so I put in his description.

After the Johnson collection I have always found the *Illustrated London News* the best hunting ground for pictures of the Victorian period. This journal, which began in 1847, is of inestimable value to the illustrator. It covers not only Britain, but foreign countries, too. Up until the invention of photogravure it was illustrated by line engraving. The very early illustrations are clearly the inventions of the artists—so that in a picture of riots in Manchester, say, the buildings are probably copied from some engraving and appropriately belligerent human figures superimposed. The later drawings would be copied from photographs. At great public ceremonies the journal commissioned artists, discreetly concealed, to sketch the event. The *Illustrated London News* came out weekly (there are two huge folio volumes for each year), and so my work was made much easier by permission to work down in the Bodleian stacks. Other illustrated journals are kept in the same area, so that I was also able to look at, say, the *Graphic* for coverage of a given event.

My third main source of pictures is the Bodleian general collection, and here I often proceed—and this goes for written material, too—in a lamentably random way. The Bodleian catalog is in two parts, one for the books printed after 1920, the other for all those before. I understand that there will some day be a complete, single one, but this has been projected for so many years that I have ceased to believe in it. Meanwhile, the pre-1920 catalog consists of the original handwritten strips of tissue that have been lightly pasted into massive tomes. Many of them are torn and flapping. Some even fall out as you open the catalog volumes. But they do provide a fascinating browsing ground, and one stumbles across extraordinary titles which one can order up, out of curiosity. A few years ago I could do this with abandon, supposing like most of the library's users that some elaborate mechanical system pulled books off the shelves and sent them on an underground railway to the readers' desks. The railway is there, but it is fed by gangs of groaning library clerks—one of whom was, for seven months, my own daughter, filling in time between school and university. Every book has to be found in an acre of bookshelves;

there are eleven floors in the stacks, each roughly an acre, each staffed by two girls. Every book has to be replaced, carefully, because if it is misplaced it disappears forever. Some of the best of my finds were made by ordering up, say, ten random volumes, of which nine would be discarded as soon as I opened them, and only the tenth would yield the nugget of gold that I hoped for. After I had heard what it felt like to collect and then replace these books, far underground, seven hours a day, I began to feel pangs about this method. But in this way I collected the greater part of the material I needed for the chapter on Sunday schools in *Childhood's Pattern*—by dint of ordering up all that the catalog offered which began with the words *Sunday school.*

From all these ramblings it is apparent that my researches have been erratic and wholly unconventional. But all the material that I shall ever need is contained in this one library, half an hour's walk from where I live. If I can't write better books about the subject I have chosen, then it is my fault; it is not the lack of resources.

REFERENCES

1. Darton, F.J. Harvey. *Children's Books in England: Five Centuries of Social Life.* 2d ed. Cambridge, Cambridge University Press, 1958, p. 175.

2. Avery, Gillian, and Bull, Angela. *Nineteenth Century Children: Heroes and Heroines in English Children's Stories, 1780-1900.* London, Hodder and Stoughton, 1965.

G—GABRIELLE A ÉTÉ GRONDÉE PAR SON GRAND-PÈRE.

H—HENRI VA PATINER SUR LA GLACE
PENDANT L'HIVER.

Children's Books and Social History

GILLIAN AVERY

For an author is is sobering to study the history of children's books. You realize then that though you may have thought you were original—that you were writing what you really thought and what you really wanted to say—you are dancing, as likely as not, to the tune of the age. And most especially does this apply to those of us who hope to win the approval of adults, of the educationalists, literary critics, child psychologists, moralists. For fashions in education and in children change rapidly, and the child hero that pleases one generation of pundits seems dismally out of date to the next, and usually completely incomprehensible to later child readers.

The heroes of the children's story of any given time show the qualities that the elders have considered desirable, attractive, or interesting in the young. Sometimes they have wanted the obedient, diligent, miniature adult, sometimes the evangelical child, or perhaps they have had a penchant for sprightly mischief, or sought to inculcate self-knowledge and independence. The surprise lies not in the swings of fashion in the pattern child, but in the unanimity of opinion at any given time abut his qualities. But the melancholy fact is that the higher the book's reputation with the educationalists and moralists of the time, the flatter does it fall with the children of succeeding generations. As social history it is fascinating; as literature it is moribund.

The children's book of the last century is a particularly fruitful field for the social historian because, especially during the Victorian period in England, the child went on being a child for such a long time, encapsulated in his own small world. Girls did not emerge from the schoolroom until seventeen or eighteen. Boys went on for even longer; their life at university was a prolonged childhood.

In this there is an enormous difference between the English and the American book. I noticed it very strongly when I was working on two little stories by Mary Howitt which I used in *The Echoing Green.* One, *The Children's Year* (1847), was an account of the day-to-day life of her own children. The other, *Our Cousins in Ohio* (1849), had been put together from the letters written by her sister who had emigrated with her family. The English children led very sheltered, childlike lives beside their American cousins. The little Howitts only played at being grownup with their toy cooking stove and their Swiss Family Robinson house. The Alderson cousins, from six-year-old Nanny to ten-year-old Willy, all had duties in a household that was far too busy to allow the children to be kept apart in their own small world. Even as a child I noticed this sturdy independence as the great difference between the English and the American book; but I was surprised at how soon, on the evidence of *Our Cousins in Ohio,* an English family would shake off old attitudes and take on the new outlook.

Presumably at the root of it lay the absence of servants. Like every prosperous European settler before her, Emma Alderson had at first wrung her hands and lamented the difficulty of finding white servants. She tried to find a woman who would help with the washing, but no one would come. She asked a poorly clad boy if he thought his mother would be willing. " 'My mother!' returned the boy, who seemed astonished, 'she can't go; and if she could she wouldn't.' " When she did manage to find a woman poor enough to consent to work for another she had to assure her repeatedly that there was no degradation in doing other people's washing. Emma Alderson said with a sigh, "as she had before done of such occasions, how different things were in old England, where there were only too many washerwomen for the linen....Another sigh she heaved, for she saw in this reluctance to do daily labour the hateful effects of slavery, which had made labour and degradation synonymous words."

Nearly every English visitor of this period remarked how Americans seemed to notice no difference in rank or class, but addressed one as an equal. Some deplored this, a few admired it, but all were astonished. The Aldersons accepted it; in their household the servants sat down to meals with the family "according to the universal custom in this country," Mary Howitt explained to English readers. Colored visitors also shared their meals, which was not a universal custom.

The existence in England of a vast servant class—and you had to be poor indeed not to have somebody to work for you, even if it was only to scrub the steps or do the washing once a month—meant that there was a tremendous difference in the juvenile book trade between England and America in the middle years of the last century. Even as late as 1887 in her pamphlet *What Books to Give and What to Lend*, Charlotte Yonge could make the distinction between drawing-room books for the leisured classes and books for the cottage home. By then the Education Act of 1870 which provided schooling for every child was taking effect, and the syllabus of the elementary school was expanding beyond the basic three Rs, but she still felt that many books written with the upper-class child in mind would be incomprehensible to the poor child. They would not enjoy works of imagination, for instance, because imagination was something wholly outside their experience. Miss Yonge said that she had found many cottage children who had never been told the old fairy stories. Books with a literary style were probably too difficult for them, and this ruled out many of Mrs. Ewing's. But there was another difficulty over and above this: the drawing-room story might introduce the cottage child to situations he could not properly understand, and lead him to envy and temptation. Take, for instance, *Tom Brown's Schooldays*. Tom Brown, the son of a country landowner, is spirited, disobedient, with a lordly indifference to other people's property—and this is as it should be; he is a fine, manly fellow who is being educated to be a leader of men; nobody would want him to be a muff. But the ethic would be very different for the child of one of his father's tenants. This is what a farmer says to a boy whom he catches stealing corn from the sheaves in the harvest fields:

> Just what I should expect. A boy begins by idling away his time, and then steals, to hide his fault. And I tell you what, you may be very thankful this has all come out. If you had escaped this time, you might have gone on stealing until you became a confirmed thief and liar—the two faults generally go together—and you might have ended your days on the gallows; think of that. Many a boy has begun a wicked life as young as you are, by stealing apples when he ought to have been at church on the Sunday, and has gone from bad to worse, till he has been hung for some dreadful crime.

There is no date to this little story, called *The Gleaners*, but I would guess that it is within ten years of *Tom Brown*, published in 1857.

There were in those days two quite distinct codes of behavior, one for the leisured classes, one for the working classes. For one thing, the cottage child had no time to play. Charlotte Yonge, who usually held that the Victorian class system was heaven-ordained, was once struck by the sadness of this. "She was thirteen," she wrote of a little nursery maid, "and all that she viewed as child's play had long been gone out of her; she could not understand her charges' fun and nonsense, or why Mrs. Gray would not have them called 'naughty' for getting their frocks torn, and their hands dirty, or for pulling all the chairs about, the very things that gave her most trouble." The little nursemaid would certainly not have been indulged like this when she was a child; but she had to endure it in the more privileged.

If we are to go by the little books published by the hundreds in early and mid-Victorian England by such bodies as the Religious Tract Society and the Society for the Promotion of Christian Knowledge, which specialized in providing Sunday school prizes, the ideal cottage child spent no time in play. Play was not sinful in itself, but might lead him to mingle with undesirable playfellows. Besides, there was no time for it, though it seemed to be generally agreed that it was more reprehensible in girls (probably because they would be more easily contaminated, and anyway they should be helping their mothers with the younger children). Boys—again this seemed to be generally agreed—had an altogether coarser and more obstinate nature, and could not be deflected from a certain amount of recreation. The ideal boy, though he might kick a ball around sometimes (he never, naturally, did anything that involved cruelty to animals, or damage to property) was sober and steady, truthful of course, ready to take orders from his superiors and to carry them out. Initiative was not required of him; ambition was deplored. He might rise from being a stable boy to the position of trusted coachman, or become a warehouse clerk (if he was a town boy) and a superintendent of a Sunday school in his spare time. Sometimes he might be helped to emigrate. The happy ending of *Froggy's Little Brother*, a very popular street-waif story published in 1875, is that Froggy, whose father, mother, and little brother have all died, is found a place in an orphanage with the promise that he will be taught the trade of carpenter. The Horatio Alger type of rags-to-riches story was absolutely unknown in England. It happened in fact—the fluidity of the English class system is a commonplace—but not in fiction.

Even less than her brother was the cottage girl allowed to cherish ambitions. Here the writers were up against great difficulty. They knew the terrible moral dangers that the young servant girl was exposed to, plunged at the age of fourteen or so into a strange household, far from those who had hitherto kept a watchful eye on her, and assailed by temptations that they could not name, perhaps not even to themselves. All that these writers could do was to admonish her to be modest, to abjure showy clothes and empty-headed frivolity. At the beginning of the century, Hannah Moore could specify exactly what happened to girls who yearned for smart clothes and fashionable company—they were seduced and staggered home with a dying baby to die themselves. Victorians could not speak out like this; their books for the cottage girl must have seemed incomprehensibly negative to the recipient—the gentry, as always, interfering and nagging. To read cottage literature is to become aware that there was no safe recreation. Dancing, singing, for girls—smoking, drinking, for boys—none of them morally wrong in themselves, and indeed permissible to those who lived in more comfortable circumstances—must all be avoided by the poor. There were grave dangers in cheap books, so they had much better read only those that their betters handed out to them. Dress and hairstyle must be of the plainest, no aping the fashions of a superior class: "If only you were to hear how foolish the gentlefolk and ladies think those girls, you would never wish to look so silly again."

Above all, a girl must not seek to rise out of her station, because this, though the writers do not say so, will make her easy prey to the gentleman seducer. The best way she can get on in the world is to become a respectable upper servant, and perhaps marry a good, steady artisan. "I am glad you can clear-starch, Sophy," says one of the adult helpers in *The Sunday School Treat to Richmond* (1860). "Strive to improve more and more, and do not be satisfied till you can wash and iron better than any one else you know; and who can tell, but in a few years you may have the great honour of being one of the clear-starchers to Her Majesty."

After the 1870s the gulf between the two types of reader did begin to close. The syllabus of the elementary school became broader, so that children could be given stories with a historical setting. The prize book became less didactic; by the 1890s boys' school stories were being handed out, depicting the boarding school life of the privileged classes where, though the behavior might be boisterous, the moral tone was good; the boys in them never lied, or sneaked, or cringed, or failed to play the game. For by the 1890s the ethic for the working-class boy had changed; those who were concerned for his welfare sought to make him healthy and manly, able to speak up for himself and look people straight in the eye. In short, they were trying to shape him more like his betters, the difference in the approach being due to the fact that England was by that time almost wholly urban, the number of country boys going to work for the local landowner having dwindled to the point that publishers no longer had to provide for them.

I—ISABELLE EST UNE PAUVRE PETITE IN-
VALIDE.

But in the middle years of the century, there was one type of book that did cut right across the classes and was read by drawing-room and cottage child alike. This was the evangelical story, and its popularity was immense. By the 1880s stories of slum children who died joyfully repeating some sacred text were being handed out in the hundreds of thousands as Sunday school prizes and were the required Sunday reading in prosperous homes. And there was Mrs. Sherwood, whose *Fairchild Family* I mentioned in the previous paper. Born in 1775, all her important works were written in the pre-Victorian era, but she dominated the Victorian Sunday. Herself an evangelical, her books were found in High Church and Low Church home alike. She united the duke's children with the young servants, the intellectual High Anglican home with the Manchester semidetached villa at a time when there was deep distrust, even hatred, for shades of religious opinion that differed from one's own, and an enormous gulf between drawing room and cottage—as we have seen. She welded herself to Victorian respectability; her stories were as much a part of English childhood as the *Bibliothèque rose* was of the well-conducted little French citizen. Every Victorian who recalled his childhood reading named Mrs. Sherwood. Dickens in *Little Dorrit* makes Arthur Clennam recall with horror the Sundays of his youth and the dreary little tracts he was obliged to read, which anyone can recognize as of the type that Mrs. Sherwood or her sister Mrs. Cameron wrote.

But evangelical literature for the young changed dramatically during the last century. Take the attitude to personal appearance alone. At the beginning of the century vanity was regarded as so deadly a sin, so much to be discouraged, that the looks of the characters were never described, except to say, perhaps, that though their faces were so plain, their natures were so good that everybody loved them. But by the 1880s the Religious Tract Society was publishing stories in which little girls with curly golden hair, violet eyes, and pearly teeth used their winning appearance to good effect, to bring light into the dark, cold, hardened souls of the adults around them.

The very fact that fiction was permissible in the evangelical home at all showed a change of thinking. Works of imagination were at one time anathema—they were all lies, and it made no difference that some purported to be improving. The evangelical of this cast of mind would have given his child some such compilation of true accounts of the lives of godly children, as James Janeway's *A Token for Children*, "being an Exact Account of the Conversion, Holy and Exemplary Lives and Joyful Deaths of Several Young Children." James Janeway was a seventeenth-century puritan divine who first preached in London in the plague year, 1665, and had his own meeting house in Rotherhithe. He died young, at the age of thirty-eight, in 1674. *A Token for Children* was first published in 1672 and was imitated time and time again in other anthologies of the holy lives and deaths of children. You have to remember that for many evangelical families it would be the only book that a child might read, along with the Bible, Foxe's *Martyrs*, and *Pilgrim's Progress*. It was the unvarnished truth, there was no fiction about it. Janeway had said in his preface: "What is presented is faithfully taken from experienced solid Christians, some of them no way related to the children, who themselves were eye and ear witnesses of God's works of wonder, or from reverend godly ministers, and from persons that are of unspotted reputation for holiness, integrity, and wisdom."

We catch a glimpse, though a fictitious one, of how Janeway was received in *The Sunday Scholars' Magazine or Monthly Reward Book*. (This little periodical seems to have been born and died in one year, 1821.) The Sunday school teacher comes to visit a cottage home and finds one of his scholars reading *A Token for Children*, and expresses the hope that he will become like "those children of whose holy lives and happy deaths you read in that good book." The mother becomes tearful at these words. "Ah sir, that's what I'm afraid of; for the best seem always to go first, and now my poor boy is become so good, I sometimes fear I shall lose him, too, and I can't bear the thought of it. But to be sure it is the most entertaining book that can be. Night after night, as soon as ever Tom comes home from work, he helps me turn the mangle, and then gets to his book; we be never tired of it."

"The most entertaining book that can be"—I think this is an important point. We have to think ourselves back into the position of children like Tom: sweated labor during the day, precious little comfort when he got home, starved of all books of imagination, knocked about by his elders, no doubt—and here in Janeway he finds first a heavenly peace, and secondly a dignity for children which is denied to them in health; he finds children the center of awed interest, children uttering words of wisdom which all listen to with riveted attention, children rebuking their elders unrebuked, children urging their brothers and sisters to repentance, children exhorting, comforting. It is not difficult to imagine how children—not just laboring boys, either—might have ecstasies of daydreaming with themselves playing the central figures in these dramas. And I think that Janeway's book, and similar compilations, did have a very important effect on writers brought up on them as children. I would even guess that the boy Dickens was comforted by such daydreams when he felt bitterly that he was an outcast, thrown out by his family into a hostile and uncaring world, and that these later took shape in the deaths of, for instance, Paul Dombey and Nell.

Death played the central part in the education of the young evangelical. Those responsible for their upbringing felt that their most solemn charge was to secure what they called "early piety," that is, a change of heart in the child, a realization of his utterly sinful nature, his total depravity. Solemnly and persistently, in tracts, sermons, and hymns, writers and preachers tried to drive this home to children, together with the inevitability of death and the ghastliness of the punishment that awaited the unregenerate.

"Could a lost soul drop but one tear, once in ten thousand years," John Pike, an early nineteenth-century Baptist pastor wrote in his *Persuasions to Early Piety*, "and do this till a sea as vast as all the seas on earth together were filled with tears, all its sufferings in that long, long period would be but the beginning of eternal misery. All those millions of years of wretchedness would bring the unhappy soul no nearer to an end of its torments than one fleeting hour. O infinitely miserable creature! that when millions of years of sorrow are past, can only say, those flames again, these tortures again!' "

The child of evangelical parents was taken to funerals, to deathbeds, to executions even, and sometimes to condemned cells. Time was so short, eternity yawned beyond the grave; the evangelicals could not bear to see their children wasting the precious moments and letting life drift by, and they continually searched their minds for methods to shock them into seriousness. Annie Keary, the author of *Father Phim*, remembered a little book called *The Warning Clock*. (This in fact was written by Mrs. Cameron, the sister of Mrs. Sherwood, in 1829.) It began with a picture of a little girl in bed, a clock on the wall of her room, and an old nurse drawing aside the bed curtain. The child wakes and says, "Call me again, nurse, in an hour's time, then I will get up." Thus it goes on all day, till midnight comes. Then there was a picture of the clock pointing to twelve, in the doorway a man with a veiled face, of whom the story said that "he would brook no delay," and the child sitting up in bed at last, but with an expression of agony on her face. Mrs. Sherwood wrote *A Drive in the Coach through the Streets of London* (1818) about a mother who takes her vain little daughter for a drive and allows her to make one purchase from every shop they pass, stipulating only that no shop passed may be passed by, and that every object should be put to its proper purpose. The little girl enjoys herself tremendously, and prattles about the lovely things she has bought. And then the carriage draws up to the coffin-maker's shop. Her mother need say nothing, the point has been made.

The early nineteenth-century Sunday school magazines were full of somber warnings, too:

> My dear children, the whooping cough is spreading fast; several little ones have died of it. Day after day I hear the bell tolling, and one little child after another has been buried here; and as I walk out into the villages and the lanes, and go into the schools I see your little faces swelled and hear you coughing, but I am pained to think how few of you would be found ready were you called to die of it. Let me beg of you, dears, to try to think about death; say to yourselves, "perhaps I may soon die, and then where will my soul go? Will it go to heaven, or will it be cast down into hell, where there will be weeping and wailing and gnashing of teeth?"

The evangelical child had been given actual examples of holy deaths, little tract stories about death that had come to heedless, unthinking children as a punishment, or to good ones as a reward. But *The Fairchild Family* was the first full-length novel that had been written for them. You have to bear in mind all the elements of an eighteenth-

century evangelical education when you look at this book—the reiter-
ated, somber warnings, the visits to deathbeds, the dwelling on eternal
punishment, the morals drawn from every incident in daily life. But even
so, one cannot deny that it is unique. It was never imitated, never
repeated; not even Mrs. Sherwood herself attempted to do so. It is the
story of little Lucy, Emily, and Henry Fairchild, aged nine, eight, and six
when the first part was published in 1818 (though they were not appreci-
ably older in 1847, when the third part appeared), their religious education, the lessons they learn from their own naughtinesses and from the
misfortune of others. This is one element of an evangelical education of a
sort which was commonplace in the early years of the last century. But
Mrs. Sherwood was clearly influenced by the Gothic novels of her youth,
so there is, over and above the evangelical preoccupation with
deathbeds, lavish descriptions of graveyards, and vaults and coffins and
bones. And superimposed on all this, the three delightfully lifelike
children—perhaps the first credible child characters that had appeared
in the juvenile book. Or rather, they oscillate between being lifelike (and
naughty) and glib little puppets who shake their heads solemnly about
the spiritual shortcomings of others.

Every sort of death used by the evangelicals occurs in *The Fairchild
Family*. There is death used as a punishment: Miss Augusta Noble
disobeys her parents and lights a candle so she can admire herself in the
looking glass, and burns to death. (She is punished thereby both for
disobedience and for vanity.) There is death as a warning: Mr. Fairchild
finds his children quarreling and takes them to a gibbet with the corpse
of a man who has murdered his brother hanging from it. They go to visit
the corpse of their old gardener, which is described in much detail (Mrs.
Sherwood throughout the book is morbidly preoccupied with the physical aspect of death and the smell of corruption). The children also go to
witness the death of a good little boy, Charley Trueman. This child had
played an important part in bringing little Henry Fairchild back to the
fold of the righteous when he had fallen heavily from grace by disobeying
his father. He had achieved this by describing how very horrible the
vaults were in the church, and the coffins they contained. The death of
Charley Trueman is so characteristic of this type of exemplar deathbed,
to be found in Janeway and hundreds of other evangelical works, that it is
worth quoting here in full:

> Poor little Charley was lying on a bed in his grandmother's room. His
> head was lying on a pillow, supported by his mother, who sat upon the
> bed looking at her dying child, whilst the tears ran down her cheeks.
> John Trueman was kneeling on one side of the bed, holding one of
> Charles's hands. Mr. Somers [the clergyman] stood looking silently on,

sometimes lifting up his eyes and repeating something to himself, as if in prayer; and Mary Bush, and poor Charles's elder brother and sister, were crying in different parts of the room.

When Mr. and Mrs. Fairchild with the children came in, Charles's eyes were shut, and he lay as if sleeping. He was very much changed since the day before: his eyes were sunk, his face become deadly pale, and his mouth drawn close. When Henry looked at him, he could keep his tears back no longer; they overflowed his eyes, and ran fast down his cheeks. After a few minutes, Charles opened his eyes, and looked round him at every one. At length, perceiving Henry, he smiled and put his hand towards him.

"Dear, dear Charles!" said Henry, sobbing.

"Do not cry, Master Henry," said Charles, speaking in a low voice; "I am happy."

"And what makes you happy now, my dear boy?" said Mr. Somers: "speak and tell us, that we may all here present lay fast hold of the same hope, which is able to make a dying bed so easy." [This catechising of the dying features in all exemplar deathbeds. It was done so that the answers could uplift and be remembered by the living.]

Charles turned his dying eyes towards Mr. Somers, and answered: "I know that my Redeemer liveth; and though after my skin worms shall destroy this body, yet in my flesh I shall see God." (Job xix, 25, 26.) [Dickens in *Little Dorrit* spoke savagely of the type of tract "with a parenthesis in every other line with some such hiccuping reference as Ep. Thess. c. iii v. 6 and 7."]

The little boy spoke these words with difficulty: and indeed the latter part was rather guessed at than heard distinctly: then, as if quite worn out, he shut his eyes, and lay as much as an hour as if asleep, though his frequent startings and convulsions, with his slow and solemn breathings, showed that death was coming on apace. At length he awoke, and his mother and Mr. Somers spoke to him, but he took no notice of them. The manner of his breathing changed: he looked round the room eagerly; then suddenly looking upwards, and fixing his eyes on one corner of the room, the appearance of his countenance changed to a kind of heavenly and glorious expression, the like of which no one present ever before had seen; and every one looked towards the place on which his eyes were fixed, but they could see nothing extraordinary. After a while his eyes half shut, and he fell into the agonies of death.

Death, even the death of those whose souls are redeemed, is a dreadful sight; for the sinful body struggles hard with it. Satan then does his worst; but it is written, "He that is with us is stronger than he that is against us;" and he will surely deliver those whom he hath purchased with his precious blood even from the power of death and hell.

After several convulsive pangs, little Charles stretched himself; he breathed slower and slower and slower; then, fetching a deep sigh, his features became fixed in death. Nurse, who had come into the room some time before, perceiving that the soul of the dear child was departed, came up to the bedside, and gently closed the eyes, and bound up with a handkerchief the mouth of the corpse; and having laid the arms and feet straight upon the bed, she stepped back to wipe away the tears that were running fast down her cheeks. All this while no one spoke, but all stood silently looking on the features of the dear child as they settled in death. After a few moments, Mr. Somers gave notice that he was going to pray, and every one knelt down around the bed. Mr. Somers's prayer was very short, but it was very solemn; he first gave God thanks for the happy departure of the dear child, now with Christ his Redeemer; and, secondly, he earnestly prayed that God would, in his appointed time, grant unto all then present an equally happy death. His prayer finished with these words: "May we die the death of the righteous, and may our latter end be like his."

J—JACQUES S'AMUSE TOUTE LA JOURNÉE AVEC SES JOUJOUX.

What was the effect on the child reared in the first decades of the nineteenth century of this sort of literature—Janeway, Sherwood, and their followers? You have to bear in mind that imaginative literature for the young at this time was nonexistent, that fairy tales were outlawed. I have said that I think it may have influenced Dickens when he came to record the deaths of Paul Dombey and little Nell. It certainly affected the children's writers of the second half of the century. Whatever Janeway and Sherwood did to Dickens, certainly all three of them had a mesmeric effect upon those who came after. In some of the books there was still an evangelical element—they were using the death of children to drive home a message—but again and again, one senses in the writers of the 1860s onward that they were using death to draw tears, that they prided themselves on making their readers weep.

Paul Dombey's death certainly infected Florence Montgomery with the urge to imitate it in *Misunderstood* in 1869. This was a very influential book in its way and set a fashion for misunderstood children for many decades to come. Humphrey and Miles are the motherless sons of a wealthy baronet, Sir Everard. Humphrey, volatile and thoughtless, is always leading little Miles, a delicate child, into mischief. Miles, the image of his mother who died of consumption, is the baronet's favorite, and Humphrey is rejected as an unloving, unaffectionate child who does not care a jot for anybody. But Humphrey yearns for affection, senses that his father prefers Miles, and creeps for comfort to the portrait of his mother, trying to fancy that her arms are round him and her shoulder against his head. Alas, Humphrey leads his little brother into mischief once too often. In flagrant defiance of his father he climbs a forbidden tree, falls from a rotten branch and, of course, suffers some fearful spinal injury, while Miles recovers. Humphrey is brought into the drawing-room, where his mother's portrait hangs, and there he dies with his eyes upon her. Sir Everard, too late, realizes the treasure he has lost. You will be glad to hear that I do not propose to quote you the death scene, for this occupies eighty pages of a 300-page book. It shamelessly follows Paul Dombey's death, even to the sound of the rushing waters. "'Has God sent you to fetch me at last, mother?' he cries. 'Oh, mother, I'll come, I'll come.' And Humphrey has gone to join her."

The interesting point about this book is how the ideal of juvenile behavior has changed since Mrs. Sherwood's time. Then disobedience was the cardinal fault, especially disobedience of one's father. One of the most somber moments in *The Fairchild Family* occurs when Henry refuses to learn his Latin lesson. (His reason for refusing, which he admits to the servant, though not to his father, is that if he learns this one, it will only be succeeded by another, and then another even harder, and he is frightened.) Mr. Fairchild's wrath is terrible indeed; Henry is flogged and then banished, so to speak, into outer darkness, with his father's voice ringing in his ears: "I stand in place of God to you, whilst you are a child." Everybody turns from him, nobody is allowed to speak to him. In *Misunderstood* Humphrey also has disobeyed his father, and in books of an earlier epoch his death would be used by the author to show what the results of disobedience are. Florence Montgomery, however, uses the death of Humphrey to punish the father who has not taken enough trouble to understand the child. It should be remembered that she did not originally intend *Misunderstood* for children, though it was at once treated as a children's book and had a great influence on those that were written after.

Misunderstood, with the unashamed pleasure that its author took in depicting beautiful children in beautiful surroundings, could be said to represent one aspect of a reaction against what one might call the evangelical cult of ugliness, the feeling that ugliness made for moral safety and rectitude—not just in Protestant churches, which shuddered with horror at the thought of the sensual practices of Latin nations, but in everyday life. One can take as an example the furnishings of the 1850s and 1860s, with their emphasis on heavy solidity. There was a feeling that secular ugliness was seemly—and this was the mood of Carlyle, whom we might call a secular Calvinist. This dour, forbidding ethos at its most extreme can be found in the passages about Mrs. Clennam in *Little Dorrit.* There, the grimness of the surroundings seems to be an essential part of Mrs. Clennam's grim beliefs.

This was to change. Carlyle was to be superseded as prophet and sage by Pater and Ruskin; the Tractarians and Ritualists brought softness and beauty into the churches; and writers felt free to indulge senses which perhaps had been starved in their childhood. One of those whom it affected was Mrs. Ewing, and it is interesting to contrast her attitude toward writing for children with that of her mother, Margaret Gatty. Mrs. Gatty was born in 1809, her daughter Juliana Horatia in 1841. Mrs. Gatty had had a lighthearted Regency youth, but by the time she had children of her own, she was an early Victorian in spirit and conformed to the ethic of the age; she wrote stories which feature her family, shown listening dutifully to the sister they nickname Aunt Judy (this is intended to be Juliana Horatia), who delivers little homilies about their behavior, draws morals from the incidents and accidents of their daily life, and is in short—as my great aunt would have said—"prosy and preachy to a degree, my dear." (Incidentally, it is interesting to find in Juliana Horatia's journals that though she did indeed tell stories to her younger brothers and sisters, they were apparently spine-chilling murder serials that went on night after night.) Mrs. Gatty's attitude toward her writings for children was much the same as Mrs. Sherwood's; she felt that they must all contain moral truth, that this must be their purpose. In the desolate little story called *Rabbits' Tails*, she makes the narrator hesitate before she tells it: "There was something sad about the story. There was no exact teaching to be got out of it."

By the time Juliana Horatia Ewing wrote for children, scruples such as these could be cast aside. She did not need to consider whether the story she chose to tell provided a basis for moral or religious teaching.

Many of them, in fact, do; she was as devoted a churchwoman as her mother. But by the 1880s, the mood of the times allowed her to introduce pathetic incidents for their own sake—and she admitted, even boasted, how she enjoyed making her readers cry. In this she was like scores of her contemporaries. Edward Salmon, in an 1886 article on "What Girls Read" in the journal *Nineteenth Century*, complained: "The teaching which comes of girls' books amounts to this. If you are wicked you must reform, and when you have reformed you will die! Good young people are not allowed to see many years of life."

I have chosen one of Mrs. Ewing's death scenes to illustrate how far the later Victorians departed from the evangelical death, though the original influence was from this type of literature. They loved to make beautiful children die. It did not seem to occur to them how nihilistic their attitude was. They presented youth, full of hope and promise, only to destroy it for the sole purpose of drawing tears. Mrs. Ewing's *The Story of a Short Life*, published in 1885, the year of her death, is typical of its time for its preoccupation with childish beauty and noble birth. Leonard is the only child of a wealthy, fastidious, dilettante baronet. He becomes passionately absorbed in the affairs of the nearby military camp, falls from his mother's carriage at a review there, suffers some unspecified spinal injury, fades away in the beauty of his youth, enduring his pain and weakness by pretending he is a wounded soldier. In the end he is carried to the camp at his urgent request, because he wants to die like a soldier. We see him in his radiant beauty in a variety of poses: "with coloured rays from coats of arms in the stained glass panes on his fair hair"; or, standing beside the Van Dyck portrait of his ancestor Rupert, the cavalier, eyes liquid with tears; or, "in a holiday suit of crimson velvet with collars and ruffles of old lace, his rose-leaf cheek laid against the black head of Sweep, his puppy." And later, on his sickbed, he is described as "a vision of rare beauty, beautifully dressed, with crippled limbs lapped in Eastern embroideries by his colour-loving father, his wan face and wonderful eyes lambent with an intelligence so eager and wistful, that the creature looked less like a morsel of suffering humanity than a soul fretted by the brief detention of an all-but-broken chain."

And so Leonard has to die. His last request is that his special friend, the officer who has won the Victoria Cross, should stand outside the chapel of the camp at evening service and sing the hymn that Leonard has chosen while the soldiers sing it inside. This hymn is known as the "Tug-of-War Hymn" because the congregation invariably tries to pull away from the organist.

> In the Barrack Master's hut my hero lay dying. His mind was now
> absolutely clear, but during the night it had wandered—wandered in a

delirium that was perhaps some solace of his sufferings, for he had believed himself to be a soldier on active service, bearing the brunt of battle and the pain of wounds; and when fever consumed him, he thought it was the heat of India that parched his throat and scorched his skin, and called again and again in noble raving to imaginary comrades to keep up heart and press forward.

About four o'clock he sank into stupor, and the Doctor forced Lady Jane to go and lie down, and the Colonel took his wife away to rest also.

At gun-fire Leonard opened his eyes. For some minutes he gazed straight ahead of him, and [his father], who sat by his bedside, could not be sure whether he were still delirious or no; but when their eyes met he saw that Leonard's senses had returned to him, and kissed the wan little hand that was feeling about for the The Sweep's head in silence that he almost feared to break.

Leonard broke in by saying, "When did you bring Uncle Rupert to Camp, Father dear?"

"Uncle Rupert is at home, my darling; and you are in Uncle Henry's hut."

"I know I am; and so is Uncle Rupert. He is at the end of the room there. Can't you see him?"

"No, Len. I only see the wall, with your text on it that poor old Father did for you."

"My 'Goodly heritage' you mean? I can't see that now. Uncle Rupert is in front of it. I thought you put him there. Only he's out of his frame, and—it's very odd!"

"What's odd, my darling?"

"Some one has wiped away all the tears from his eyes."

"Hymn two hundred and sixty-three: 'Fight the good fight of faith.' "

As nine hundred and odd men rose to their feet with some clatter of heavy boots the V.C. turned quietly out of the crowded church, and stood outside upon the steps, bare-headed in the sunshine of St. Martin's little summer, and with the tiniest of hymn books between his fingers and thumb, and lifting his face towards the Barrack Master's hut, he sang—as he rarely sang in drawing rooms, even words the most felicitous to melodies the most sweet—sang not only to the delight of dying ears, but so that the Kapellmeister [at the organ] heard him, and smiled as he heard.

> The son of God goes forth to war,
>   A kingly crown to gain;
> His blood-red banner streams afar:
>   Who follows in his train?
>
> Who best can drink His cup of woe
>   Triumphant over pain,
> Who patient bears His cross below,
>   He follows in His train.

On each side of Leonard's bed, like guardian angels, knelt his father and mother. At his feet lay The Sweep, who now and then lifted a long, melancholy nose and anxious eyes.

At the foot of the bed stood the Barrack Master. He had taken up this position at the request of [Leonard's father], who had avoided any further allusion to Leonard's fancy that their Naseby ancestor had come to Asholt Camp, but had begged his big brother-in-law to stand there and blot out Uncle Rupert's ghost with his substantial body.

Near the window sat Aunt Adelaide, with her prayer-book, following the service in her own orderly and pious fashion, sometimes saying a prayer aloud at Leonard's bidding, and anon replying to his oft-repeated inquiry: "Is it the third Collect yet, Aunty dear?"

She had turned her head, more quickly than usual, to speak, when, clear and strenuous on vocal stops, came the melody of the "Tug-of-war hymn."

"There; there it is! Oh, good Kapellmeister! Mother dear, please go to the window and see if V.C. is there, and wave your hand to him. Father dear, lift me up a little, please. Ah, now I hear him! Good V.C.! I don't believe you'll sing better than that when you're promoted to be an angel. Are the men singing pretty loud? May I have a little of that stuff to keep me from coughing, Mother dear? You know I am not impatient; but I do hope, please God, I shan't die till I've just heard them *tug* that verse once more!"

The sight of Lady Jane had distracted the V.C.'s thoughts from the hymn. He was singing mechanically, when he became conscious of some increasing pressure and irregularity in the time. Then he remembered what it was. The soldiers were beginning to tug.

In a moment more the organ stopped, and the V.C. found himself, with over nine hundred men at his back, singing without accompaniment, and in unison.

> A noble army—men and boys,
> 　The matron and the maid,
> Around their Saviour's throne rejoice,
> 　In robes of white arrayed.

The Kapellmeister conceded that verse to the shouts of the congregation; but he invariably reclaimed control over the last.

Even now, as the men paused to take breath after their "tug" the organ spoke again, softly but seraphically, and clearer and sweeter above the voices behind him rose the voice of the V.C., singing to his little friend—

> They climbed the steep ascent of Heaven,
> 　Through peril, toil and pain—

the men sang on; but the V.C. stopped, as if he had been shot. For a man's hand had come to the Barrack Master's window and pulled the white blind down.

What should be noticed about this death scene is that though it physically resembles the Janeway deathbeds, or Mrs. Sherwood's account of the death of little Charles Trueman, with the sorrowing relations clustered round the bed, weeping and listening to the child's last words, and though there seems to be a vaguely religious air about it—the soldiers are singing a hymn as Leonard dies—it is, in fact, wholly secular; Leonard is concerned not with the words but with hearing the soldiers whom he hero-worships singing them. *The Story of a Short Life* is piece of self-indulgence on Mrs. Ewings's part, at a time when she was ill, separated from her soldier husband who was in Malta, and filled with nostalgic longing (strange as this may seem) for army life, probably wistful, too, for the sort of comfort and loving attention that lapped her hero on his sickbed. And at the back of her mind lingered the evangelical stories she had read as a child, which had such a compelling influence on so many writers.

And this, for me, is one of the most fascinating things about the study of children's books: the way that one can detect in them the books that moved their authors when they themselves were children, and how many of these mingle with memories of their own childhood, and are overlaid with the fashionable approach of the moment.

K —K EST LA LETTRE QUE JEAN TIENT SOUS LA MAIN.

L—LOUISE DONNE DES LÉGUMES À SES
PETITS LAPINS.

Reflections on Histories of Childhood

WALTER L. ARNSTEIN

My topic, according to the program, is "Research Studies About Childhood," though I have been tempted to amend that to read "Fools Rush In Where Angels Fear to Tread." When invited to undertake this assignment, I was tempted to explain that my qualifications for the task most resembled those of the applicant for the post of governess who was asked whether she had had any previous experience working with children. "Madam," she declared, "I was a child myself for many years."

Historians are, however, supposed to be jacks of all trades—we'll skip the corollary for the moment—and, if one surveys all the works of professional historians of the past century, one does indeed find books dealing with childhood, just as one finds books dealing with constitutions, economic treaties, social reforms, and the history of clothing. Yet it is fair to observe that, until very recently, the topic of childhood was not part of the mainstream of either general comprehensive histories or of more specifically social histories.

41

In most history books, it seems fair to conclude, children were seldom seen and hardly ever heard. Part of the explanation may well lie in the fact that (in the words of Philippe Ariès): "Social phenomena such as family, love, and death are located...at a level very near the biological basis of our being, at the boundary between the biological and the mental. Only recently have we begun to understand that they change, but change very slowly, so slowly that their transformations have until now eluded the perception of contemporaries."[1] Historians have necessarily found it easier to generalize about those aspects of the past—political convictions, religious beliefs, economic exchanges—which were consciously put into words than about those which were so much taken for granted as rarely or never to be articulated or recorded.

Thus, if one seeks information about "childhood" in two volumes of essays about Samuel Johnson's England, edited by A.S. Turberville in 1933,[2] one is likely to find snippets of information in an essay entitled "Poverty, Crime, Philanthropy," or another called "Manners, Meals, and Domestic Pastimes," or yet others entitled "Sports and Games" and "Education, Schools, and Universities"; but subjects such as the place of the child in the society and assumptions regarding the proper manner of child rearing slip between the cracks. The same uncertainty about where the "history of childhood" fits into the world of scholarship seems to afflict librarians who, under Mr. Dewey's regime at any rate, scatter the volumes among the 000s, 100s, 300s, 600s, and 900s.

I have no desire to suggest that the readers of general histories will never run into children. Readers of general histories of Britain will encounter a few chimney sweeps and a few royal children—Queen Anne's fourteen (who all died) and Queen Victoria's nine (who all lived to adulthood)—and other children who went to Sunday school and who, as of 1833, were no longer allowed to work in textile factories until they were nine years old, and who, as of 1842, were not allowed to work at all in underground mines. Scattered tidbits rather than systematic incorporation of materials has been the historical order of the day.

Yet in the last two decades that situation has altered a good deal. Family history has become very much the rage, and at some historical conferences, the program topics have come to resemble the old lifeboat slogan: "women and children first." Let me suggest three reasons for such a change:

1. A new generation of historians has sought new fields to conquer. Few graduate students desire to chip away for a decade or a lifetime at a mine from which their advisors extracted most of the gold years before.
2. Such concern with family history is characteristic of the fact that our interest in the past grows out of specific preoccupations of the present:

thus Victorians obsessed with political reform in their own day indus-
triously traced the evolution of the British constitution back to the
Middle Ages; thus victims of the interwar Great Drepression became
absorbed with economic history; thus Americans, who in 1945 discovered that the end of World War II had left the Soviet Union as one of the
world's two most powerful nations, became interested in the founding of
Russian centers and in the tracing of Russia's muscovite past; thus in the
past two decades, the civil rights movement gave rise to a widespread
concern with Afro-American history; and yet more recently, the
women's movement has spawned an even greater interest in "women's
history." A related concern that the family is breaking up or that, at the
very least, family relationships and assumptions have changed visibly
and even dramatically in the course of the past generation helps very
much to explain a new fascination with the manner in which families of
earlier decades, centuries, or millenia have operated—or failed to
operate.

3.   A third explanation for this emphasis upon family history lies in the
recent upsurge of two distinct historical subdisciplines.

One is the study of demography, the attempt to reconstruct on the
basis of parish registers, tax rolls, and much else both the census and the
social structures of societies that were unfamilier with census-takers
and lacked resident sociologists. It has been the so-called *annales* school
in France that has pioneered what is sometimes called total history.[3] In
recent years the Cambridge Group for the History of Population and
Social Structure has been similarly conerned with studies in family
reconstitution and household size in sixteenth- and seventeenth-
century England. The computer has, necessarily, done much to speed up
studies which, under the best of circumstances, would impress most of
us as laborious if not deadly.

A second subdiscipline is the development of psychohistory, or at
least the growth of a group of historians who seek their models in the
world of Freudian or post-Freudian psychology. It was the psychologist
Erik Erikson who, in books like *Childhood and Society* and *Young Man
Luther*,[4] shifted the emphasis of psychoanalysis from the pathological to
the healthy. It was Erikson also who, in his work, was willing to concede
that not all adult traumas could be traced back—i.e., reduced to—
infantile origins and who yet emphasized the importance of child rearing
assumptions and practices as one of the most influential elements of any
given culture. Specific psychohistorical theses have admittedly often
fared less well and relatively few have gone unchallenged—such as
Erikson's own suggestion that the fact that Sioux Indian youngsters were

breast-fed until they were two or three years old helps by itself to explain why Sioux men grew up to be generous with property.[5]

In any event, what I should like to do next is discuss four or five of the most influential works of the past two decades that touch upon the history of childhood. Many more than five works have been written, to be sure—and some of them are listed in the annotated bibliography appended to this paper—but it is fair to state that some of the less pretentious and more specialized works have been written very much in the shadow of several of the books I intend to mention. One of my considerations in discussing these books will be to ask where, if anywhere, they fit into the broad stream of historical writing.

Generally speaking, there are only four possible approaches to writing history on a large scale, on a "sweeping through the centuries" scale. One of these, and during most of American history the most popular, is what is often called the Whig interpretation of history,[6] the "every day in every way we are getting better and better" point of view—or, if not every day, then at least every decade or every century with occasional but temporary setbacks in between.

The second is in a sense the obverse, and until recently it has been unfamiliar in the United States, though less so in continental Europe. It is the Tory approach—the "since Adam and Eve in the Garden of Eden it has been downhill all the way" point of view, or as the late American humorist Will Coppy once phrased it in a book title: "The Decline and Fall of Practically Everybody." It is the "once there was a Golden Age but not lately" approach to the past.

A third approach, one that originated with the hellenistic historian Ptolemy in the second century B.C., and that was revived by the Italian historian Giovanni Batista Vico in the early eighteenth century and, in different ways, by Oswald Spengler and Arnold Toynbee in the twentieth century, is the cyclical approach, the "here we go again but haven't we been this way before?" approach to the past.

A fourth approach is to see history as just one doggone thing after another, as a miscellany column in a newspaper, involving neither rhyme nor reason. Sometimes the events of the past or the present may strike us as just that way, as going neither steadily uphill nor steadily downhill nor in predictable circles—but no historian has ever made his reputation with that approach, if only because it totally lacks explanatory power. In any event we shall find that most of the new historians of childhood tend to follow either the Whig approach or the Tory approach.

The Tory or conservative approach to the history of childhood and the family in general has been more characteristic of French scholars than of American scholars, though they have recently found an American recruit. The conclusion of historians like Pierre Gaxotte and Frantz Funck-Brentano[7] is that once upon a time—two, three, or six centuries ago—there was a cohesive, stable, and orderly type of family life, supported by religion, authority, and tradition. Then along came modern society with all its ills; the ideal of domesticity fell into disrepute. Husbands and wives came to neglect one another. Children lost the habit of reverence and obedience.

Not only has the family decayed morally but, such scholars have contended, it has decayed institutionally as well. Once upon a time the family largely handled its own judicial problems. Once upon a time it was the center of property relations, as one of the prime functions and purposes of family life was to preserve the estate and to pass it on to the next generation. Once upon a time the family was an economic unit as well. On the land or in domestic industry, the father was the master of his craft, and the remaining family members served as his assistants and apprentices. Once upon a time the family was a peace-keeping force all by itself—just as the Hatfields and McCoys continued to be until a few decades ago in the Appalachian hills. In those days "the family that slayed together, stayed together."[8] Back in the Middle Ages and during the Renaissance families might be political units as well, groups engaged in dynastic rivalries.

Their conclusion, then, is that the family has not merely disintegrated morally, but that it has lost a good many of its institutional roles. There is, of course, little question that in previous centuries families more often served as economic and autonomous judicial and political units than they do in the industrialized societies of the twentieth century. For admirers of an idealized traditional society, these developments have provided more cause for regret than for rejoicing. The child used to be part of an established family structure. Now the child is only to be seen as an atom in a wider universe in which the family has lost its moorings.[9] Instead, some people have gone so far as to urge a children's "Bill of Rights" according to which children deserve the right to sue their parents, to collect a minimum wage for the chores they perform, and ultimately to choose new parents should they become dissatisfied with the old.[10]

A recent, somewhat surprising American convert to this approach is the American historian Christopher Lasch, professor of history at the University of Rochester—surprising because by temperament and by subject matter he has more often been seen as radical rather than conservative.[11] Yet in his book, *Haven in a Heartless World: The Family Besieged*,[12] Lasch has reached a conclusion very similar to that reached by French scholars, except that for Lasch it is the much-criticized American bourgeois family of only a century ago that represents the golden age from which we have descended. The nineteenth-century family, he argues, did manage for a time to provide a haven, a place protected from the wider society, a place in which children could learn from their parents how to become autonomous adults. Then not only did industrialization make it increasingly less possible for the family to remain an economic unit, but—with the best of humanitarian intentions—the state and the so-called helping professions increasingly came to invade that family autonomy. Psychiatrists, child-guidance counselors, public health officials, juvenile court officers, and experts in leisure studies have increasingly transformed the family, Lasch argues; they have taken over from parents the process of socializing children. The result, concludes Lasch, is that parents have become reluctant "to exercise authority or to assume responsibility for the child's development," thus "weakening...the psychic mechanism" through which the child could "become an autonomous adult." "The child no longer wishes to succeed the father," Lasch laments. "Instead, he wishes merely to enjoy life without his interference—without the interference of any authorities at all."[13]

This, then, has been one highly significant approach by historians, one detailing how the once-autonomous family and the children that were part of that family have increasingly lost their way.

The next question I should like to take up is the question of how the most influential book in the bibliography fits these patterns, namely Philippe Ariès's *Centuries of Childhood.*[14] Published originally in 1960 in French under the more precise title *The Child and Family Life During the Old Regime,* it was translated two years later into English. Ariès takes the vast majority of his examples from French art and literature and from books of manners, etiquette, and educational manuals—but his range is a broad one, all the way from the twelfth century to the eighteenth, with numerous concluding reflections on modern times, i.e., the past two centuries.

Ariès's theme is a compelling one, namely that although childhood as a biological fact may always have existed, childhood as a concept, as a definition, is a human cultural invention. "In medieval society," he writes, "the idea of childhood did not exist; this is not to suggest that children were neglected, forsaken or despised....As soon as the child could live without the constant solicitude of his mother [or care-taker] he belonged to adult society."[15]

Only gradually did children come to be seen as different beings in art and in literature. Only gradually were children of the aristocracy and middle classes distinguished from adults by their form of dress. This development took place in the case of boys much earlier than with girls.

Only gradually did children come to play quite different games from those of adults. Only gradually were children consciously coddled and fussed over and did they come to seem a specific form of amusement and entertainment for adults.

Only very gradually, and at the behest of several generations of priests and teachers, was the age of childhood and adolescence set aside (at least for upper- and middle-class boys) as a prolonged period of education, as a period assigned to the specific moral training and systematic discipline of such children. Only gradually, finally, was the family singled out from the wider community as a special institution designed, along with the school, to remove children from adult society. The family and school were to insulate the child from "the promiscuity imposed by the old [communal] sociability."[16] Partly as a consequence, Aries concludes, "our world is obsessed by the physical, moral and sexual problems of childhood."[17]

Ariès's is a fascinating survey, filled with insights, though Ariès has been criticized for insisting that the family was being strengthened during the very time period that other scholars had seen it as losing its semi-independent economic, judicial, and political functions. Where does he fit among the possible patterns of approaching the subject that I have sketched? The irony is that, in some ultimate sense, he too belongs among the conservatives or Tories, who see a golden age giving way to a less fortunate era. Admittedly he reverses definitions: for Ariès the Middle Ages were a remarkably carefree age of sociability, in which people were much less defined by class or sex *or age* than came to be the case among the upper and middle classes (and increasingly the lower classes as well) during the nineteenth and early twentieth centuries. Ambiguities abound in his work, but ultimately he clearly prefers the easy sociability he discerns in the Middle Ages, when children mingled freely with adults in work and leisure, to a society divided by classes, one in which families cut themselves off from a wider society all in the interest of a higher good about which Ariès is ultimately dubious. In the name of this higher good, this obsessive love of children, he concludes, children were deprived of their freedom and imprisoned in boarding schools and punished by birch rods. "The old society concentrated the maximum number of ways of life into the minimum of space and accepted...the bizarre juxtaposition of the most widely different classes. The new society, on the contrary, provided each way of life with a confined space in which...each person had to resemble a conventional model, an ideal type, and never depart from it under pain of excommunication."[18]

The time span of Ariès differs sharply from that of Lasch, as indeed does the subdivision of Western society upon which each concentrates and the manner in which each defines the significant changes that have taken place. They do ultimately agree, as do the French traditionalists I referred to earlier, that children were better off in times gone by than they are today.

In Lloyd DeMause's *History of Childhood* we find the tables turned absolutely. On the basis of a five-year research project under the sponsorship of the Association of Applied Psychoanalysis, Lloyd DeMause emerged in 1974 with a collection of essays and an introductory manifesto that disagreed almost completely with the approach of Philippe Ariès.[19] DeMause disagreed that a separate concept of childhood was invented during early modern times. He also objected to the notion that the modern family restricted the child's freedom and increased the severity of punishment.[20] The very idea that children ever spent a pleasant hour during antiquity or the Middle Ages is, indeed, anathema to DeMause. To the contrary, he argues: "The history of childhood is a nightmare from which mankind has only recently begun to awaken. The further back in history one digs, the more archaic the mode of parenting, and the more likely children are to be routinely abandoned, killed, beaten, emotionally and physically starved, and sexually abused."[21] For DeMause the history of western civilization is a tale full of sound and fury in the course of which children are almost perpetually threatened by werewolves, ghosts, and bogeymen. It is, nonetheless, a span of time that can be subdivided into a series of stages:

1. The Infanticidal Mode characterized the ancient world. Unwanted children were routinely disposed of.
2. The Abandonment Mode characterized the early and high Middle Ages. During this second age children were at least believed to have souls, though battered children and children subject to sexual abuse were still the order of the day.
3. The Ambivalent Mode characterized the era of the Renaissance and Reformation. During that time there was an increase in child instruction manuals and the "close-mother image" could occasionally be found in art.
4. Further but very limited improvement was characteristic of the Intrusive Mode of the eighteenth century. "The child raised by intrusive parents," DeMause tells us, "was nursed by the mother, not swaddled, not given regular enemas, toilet trained early, prayed with but not played with, hit but not regularly whipped, punished for masturbation, and made to obey promptly with threats and guilt as often as with other methods of punishment."[22] True empathy with children was occasionally found, and pediatrics was born.

5. During the Socialization Mode (nineteenth to mid-twentieth centuries) the raising of children became less a matter of conquering their will than of training and socializing them.

6. Only a few years ago, in the middle of the twentieth century, did DeMause's sixth mode begin, the Helping Mode, an attitude based on the proposition that at each stage of development the child knows better than its parents what it needs. Both parents do their best to empathize and to fulfill the child's expanding and particular needs but never do they discipline the child or seek to form habits or strike or scold the child. The Helping Mode, DeMause concedes, is time-consuming, because it involves the parents as the servants of the child, who grows up to be "gentle, sincere, never depressed, never imitative or group-oriented, strong-willed, and unintimidated by authority."[23]

And thus, DeMause implies, after centuries of only the most limited improvement, utopia has at least been reached during the 1970s—and to think that we should all have lived long enough to observe and to celebrate the triumph.

DeMause's theory is thus almost a caricature of a Whig interpretation, in which history moves in stages, all of which involve improvement, and in which the golden age has at last been reached. His approach also involves much use of post-Freudian psychoanalytic theory and the underlying assumption that psychogenic theory (i.e., child care) is the fundamental basis of historical evolution, the foundation upon which all else—politics and economics, religion and technology—is built.

To spread the new gospel, DeMause also launched a new journal, *The History of Childhood Quarterly,* whose early issues are filled with articles with titles like "Freud and the Discovery of Child Sexuality," "Fears of Sexual License During the English Reformation," "Infanticide in Florence," "Childhood and Adolescence Among the Thirteenth-Century Saints," and "Explosive Intimacy: Psychodynamics of the Victorian Family."[24] Somehow it all proved insufficient, however, and in 1976 the journal quietly changed its name to *The Journal of Psychohistory,* an alteration that enabled the editors to devote the entire fall 1977 issue to President Carter and articles like "Toward a Psychohistory of Jimmy Carter."[25]

It is only fair to conclude by noting that DeMause's approach has not yet won the allegiance of the vast majority of professional historians. The *American Historical Review* called his essay exasperating, his methods of sampling evidence impossible, and the way in which he ignored the cultural, economic, and demographic influences upon the manner in which any society treated its children ahistorical.[26]

At least two other historians have recently made their own contribution to the Whig interpretation of the history of childhood, the belief that the quality of family life and the treatment of children have progressively improved. Edward Shorter, in *The Making of the Modern Family*,[27] is concerned with but two fundamental stages: the traditional family operating in Western Europe between the sixteenth and eighteenth centuries and the modern family. During "the bad old days," argues Shorter, custom prevailed over creativity, marriage was based on calculation rather than sentiment, and mothers treated their children with indifference.

Then came modernization, and a great "surge of sentiment" revolutionized the "sad little world" of traditional society. The nuclear family withdrew from the wider society and became the focus of a "revolution in sentiment." Husbands and wives became affectionate to each other. They married for love rather than for money. The same "revolution in sentiment" also led to good mothering. Infanticide became increasingly rare in Europe after 1750. City mothers no longer gave their children to wet nurses in the countryside but took care of them themselves. For Shorter the modern family optimistically fits modern times, times which he also identifies with the joys of the sexual revolution of our day.[28] "With the publication of *The Making of the Modern Family*," writes one less-than-friendly critic, "Shorter has established himself as the Helen Gurley Brown of social history."[29]

Lawrence Stone is a better-known and more respected scholar than Edward Shorter. Indeed, as Dodge Professor of History at Princeton University, Stone is in many respects the most eminent historian to have ventured into the burgeoning history of childhood and the family. His book, *The Family, Sex, and Marriage in England, 1500-1800*,[30] has been widely reviewed and, with significant exceptions, favorably reviewed on both sides of the Atlantic. Stone sternly rejects the kind of simplistic dualism between the old-fashioned traditional family and the progressive modern family that is postulated by Shorter. And indeed, the climax of Stone's work, the eighteenth century, coincides with the very century with which Shorter's work begins. And yet there is a curious coincidence, namely that Stone, too, has postulated a series of progressive stages in the evolution of the family.

For Stone the sixteenth century was dominated by what he calls the Open Lineage Family, the bad old days when "child-rearing practices ...tended to create special psychological characteristics in adults: suspicion towards others, proneness to violence, and an incapacity to develop strong emotional ties to any one individual....Children were neglected, brutally treated, and even killed."[31] During the next stage (the seventeenth century), that of the Restricted Patriarchal Nuclear Family, Puritanism and changes in the law combined to produce a greater degree of concern with the treatment and care of children. It was the great age of the whip, though, paradoxically, "this was the first result of a great interest in children."[32]

By the time we reach the third stage, that of the Closed Domesticated Nuclear Family of the eighteenth century, we have moved to the world of what Stone calls "affective individualism." Now marriages were based on mutual love, and children were cherished and central to the life of a family largely cut off from the rest of society. Stone goes on to postulate, but not to discuss in detail, two additional stages: the patriarchal Victorian family which he sees as a partial return to stage two, and an affective-individualist-permissive twentieth-century family which he sees as a partial return to the eighteenth-century family. However much Stone may criticize other theorists, and however much fascinating detail he may cram into over 800 pages, he, too, clearly takes a Whig approach. Step by step, with occasional setbacks, we move from cruelty and callousness to affection, companionship, and concern for children's welfare.

At this point it may be appropriate to begin the process of reflecting upon some of the books and approaches that I have been discussing, whether they involve the conservative "down from a traditional golden age" assumption or variants of a Whiggish "up to modernity" assumption.

One conclusion emerges clearly enough. Historians who have sought to survey the subject of the history of childhood on a large scale not only do not agree with one another, but they often disagree upon the most obvious fundamentals. We are faced with the most astonishing degree of diversity. Thus Lawrence Stone's age of affective individualism turns out to be the same as DeMause's Intrusive Mode and Shorter's traditional society and Ariès's schoolboy prison. The restrictive modern family of the nineteenth century that Ariès postulates proves to be Lasch's "haven in a heartless world" and Stone's revived authoritarian patriarchal family.

The major problem appears to be that far too many historians have been playing the old children's game, "Take a Giant Step." They have been striding when they ought to have been crawling—in part, no doubt, because scholars who take giant steps have more attention paid to them and sell more books. Yet as Joseph Kett of the University of Virginia has justly observed: "One of the hallmarks of this burgeoning field has been the tendency of its practitioners to write books of synthesis even though there are relatively few monographic studies to draw upon."[33]

Ariès's useful cautionary note has often been disregarded: namely, that in almost all societies of which we know, attitudes toward family and love would appear to belong to a level of thinking and assumption at which the psychological can hardly be separated from the biological. Human attitudes involving these realms have been far less likely to exist at the same level of consciousness as do, say, religious doctrines, or political and philosophical ideas. The evidence is always likely, therefore, to involve circumstantial subtleties rather than being proclaimed from the housetops for the benefit of the subsequent historian.

Yet rather than acting in a more cautious manner than when writing about well-charted historical fields, too many scholars seem to have thrown caution to the winds. Often, indeed, they appear to be unaware of the fact that they might be embarking on their research investigations guided by powerful but unarticulated ideological assumptions. As Carl Pletsch commented after reviewing the DeMause collection of essays on *The History of Childhood,* "all the authors are impervious to the possibility that mid-twentieth century white middle-class American child rearing is not abstractly superior to the behavior which they describe."[34] The very type of study that is intended to supersede parochialism often turns out to exemplify that very parochialism.

A central problem, which tends to become ever more troublesome the further back into the past a historian ventures, is that he often finds himself generalizing on the basis of very limited evidence, at times on the basis of only a single reference. Thus Lawrence Stone has been criticized for postulating the existence of the custom of courtship bundling in eighteenth-century England without finding one bit of evidence dating back to the century he is discussing.[35] Thus David Hunt has been criticized for drawing conclusions for all of French society from one admittedly highly valuable document written by the royal physician which describes the upbringing of one presumably typical Frenchman, the future King Louis XIV.

Even before the study of the history of childhood became commonplace, I used to amuse my students by telling them about the upbringing of the eighteenth-century English politician, Charles James Fox, back in the 1750s. There is no question that his father believed in unlimited indulgence. Nothing was ever to stand between a child and his happiness. A child was never to receive a command. According to the elder Fox: "Young people are always in the right, and old people in the wrong." To his children he preached: "Never do today what you can put off till tomorrow." Never "do yourself what you can get anyone else to do for you."

If young Charles wished to stamp on a gold watch or to wash his hands in a bowl of cream at dinner or to throw an office dispatch into the fire, his father said: "Very well, if you must, I suppose you must." On one occasion he had promised little Charles that he might watch a brick wall on the family estate being dynamited. He forgot the promise, and the wall was dynamited in Charles's absence. Naturally Charles was unhappy, whereupon his father had the wall rebuilt so that it might be dynamited a second time.

By the time Charles went off to public school he had become an inveterate gambler, a pastime he happily introduced among his new school friends. A fellow aristocrat said this of the father of Charles James Fox: "He educated his children without the least regard to morality, and with such extravagant vulgar indulgence, that the great change which has taken place among our youth has been dated from the time of his sons' going to Eton."[36]

The facts of this particular story are not in dispute, and it certainly provides some support for Lawrence Stone's conclusion that upper-class English parents in the eighteenth century indulged their children. The historiographical problem remains, however: how representative was this upbringing? Obviously not all English aristocrats sympathized. If temporarily characteristic of some, how long did the tendency last? If characteristic of some mid-eighteenth-century families, what possible light does it throw upon that 99 percent of the population whose sons did not attend Eton and who did not live on estates on which walls were dynamited? Such problems prove perennial in elucidating the history of childhood.

Some use of generalization in the writing of history is absolutely necessary, but one of the great difficulties among the historians of childhood has been their relative unwillingness to concede that different modes of child rearing might coexist in the same society. One significant exception to this tendency is Philip Greven, the author of *The Protestant Temperament: Patterns of Child-Rearing, Religious Experience, and the Self in Early America.*[37] Greven identifies as separate patterns of temperament the evangelicals, the moderates, and the genteel. "Evangelical family government was authoritarian, and rigorously repressive. Parental authority was absolute, and...obedience and submission were the only acceptable responses for children."[38] "Moderate families," in contrast, believed in "love and duty" rather than "love and fear"; they agreed "that children were to be obedient and loving, but they did not share the impulse to break their children's wills."[39] Greven also discerned practitioners of the "genteel mode," the gentry counterparts to Stone's affectionate English aristocrats. By the mid-eighteenth century they "had begun to rear their children in ways that would have seemed sinfully and dangerously indulgent to most moderates....Fond affection rather than conscientious discipline shaped the relationships between the generations."[40] It is useful to be reminded that previous generations resembled our own in not all raising children in identical ways, but Greven is understandably much less certain as to how many families adhered to each mode of child rearing at any given time and as to why particular modes flourished or faded.

In a sharp critique of Stone's analytical scheme, the anthropologist/ historian Alan Macfarlane asks whether "the supposed massive emotional and psychological transition" that Stone postulates for the years 1400-1800 is not imposed upon the accumulated evidence rather than flowing from that evidence. Under a slightly different set of assumptions, argues Macfarlane, "we would predict that from the very start of the period there would be some loving parents and some cruel parents, some people bringing their children up in a rigid way, others in a relaxed atmosphere, deep attachments between certain husbands and wives, frail emotional bonds in other cases. Of course there would be variations in the social and legal relations, in customs and fashions, both over time and between different socioeconomic groups," but no massive transformation.[41]

The recent upsurge of interest in the history of childhood has done a number of very useful things. It has encouraged the discovery and increased the availability of a host of different possible sources ranging from unpublished family letters, to pediatricians' observations, to wet nurses' advice, to autobiographies, to mothers' diaries, to books on child care dating back at least five centuries. Much of the evidence is fascinating but it is very partial, and often it may be quite unrepresentative, even as people who were literate at all were unrepresentative of the fifteenth, sixteenth, and seventeenth centuries. As the demographic historian Peter Laslett has written about such evidence: "So untidy is it, so variable and contradictory in its dogmas and its doctrines, so capricious in what it preserves and what it must leave out....To infer from such evidence what the whole content of the attitude to children was amongst the elite minority would itself be an uncertain task....And to attempt to go further and reconstruct on this basis the childhood experience and the childrearing practice of a whole society...would be formidable indeed."[42] Analagous reservations must unfortunately be made of the numbers and the conclusions based upon them gathered by demographic historians like Laslett.

What we can expect during the next generation is that a process of mutual criticism within the historical profession will result in a good deal of winnowing. Some conclusions about some groups in some societies in some centuries will win a wide degree of professional acceptance, and in that process both the literary evidence and the pictorial evidence, to the extent that they exist, cannot help but play a highly important role. Gillian Avery has demonstrated how significant a role literary sources must play for any persuasive social history of Victorian England. Yet I remain skeptical whether for much of the historical past we shall ever be able to do more than find a few pieces to place into a jigsaw puzzle that—at least as far as the history of childhood through the ages is concerned—will always remain tantalizingly incomplete.

A few years ago one of Lloyd DeMause's disciples, John F. Benton, wrote: "DeMause needs help. He has not yet been able to find when most (or even many) children in the past were weaned or unswaddled, or able to walk, and he has posed a challenge to historians in pointing out how much there is yet to learn about what growing up in the past was really like. I expect that help will be forthcoming and that within ten years [that is, by 1984] problems in the history of childhood which now seem insoluble for 'lack of evidence' will have their answer."[43] An interested bystander like myself—who may occasionally dip a toe into the "history of childhood" sea—finds such confidence engaging. I have no desire to discourage historians any more than literary critics from searching for their Holy Grails, but a survey of this past generation's work prompts a mood of skepticism and a note of caution. Writing the history of childhood is not child's play.

M—MARIE A DES MARGUERITES POUR SA CHÈRE MAMAN.

REFERENCES

1. Ariès, Philippe. *"The Family, Sex, and Marriage in England, 1500-1800"* (review), *American Historical Review* 83:1221, Dec. 1978.

2. Turbeville, A.S., ed. *Johnson's England*. 2 vols. Oxford, Clarendon Press, 1933.

3. *Annales: Economies, Societes, Civilisations*. Centre national de la Recherche Scientifique et l'Ecole des Hautes Etudes en Sciences Sociales. 54, Blvd. Raspail, 75006 Paris, France, 1929- .

4. Erikson, Erik. *Childhood and Society*. New York, Norton, 1950 (2d ed., 1963); and _____ . *Young Man Luther*. New York, Norton, 1958. Some possible dangers of seeking to marry psychoanalysis and history are explored *in* Jacques Barzun. *Clio and the Doctors*. Chicago, University of Chicago Press, 1974.

5. *See* Hunt, David. *Parents and Children in History*. New York, Basic Books, 1970, pp. 15-16.

6. *See* Butterfield, Herbert. *The Whig Interpretation of History*. New York, Norton, 1965.

7. Gaxotte, Pierre. *The Age of Louis XIV*. New York, Macmillan, 1970; _____ . *The French Revolution*. New York, Scribners, 1932; and Funck-Brentano, Frantz. *The Old Regime in France*. London, Edward Arnold, 1929. All three volumes have been translated from the French.

8. Stone, Lawrence. *The Family, Sex, and Marriage in England, 1500-1800*. New York, Harper & Row, 1977, p. 95.

9. Hunt, op. cit., pp. 27-31.

10. Thimmesch, Nick. "Get Ready for an International Year of Childishness!" *Chicago Tribune*, Feb. 24, 1979, p. C2, cols. 3-6.

11. *See* Lasch, Christopher. *The New Radicalism in America, 1889-1963*. New York, Knopf, 1965.

12. _____ . *Haven in a Heartless World: The Family Besieged*. New York, Basic Books, 1977.

13. Ibid., pp. 123-24.

14. Ariès, Philippe. *Centuries of Childhood: A Social History of Family Life*. New York, Knopf, 1962.

15. Ibid., p. 128.

16. Ibid., p. 413.

17. Ibid., p. 411.

18. Ibid., p. 415.

19. DeMause, Lloyd, ed. *The History of Childhood*. New York, Psychohistory Press, 1974. DeMause's article, "The Evolution of Childhood," is reprinted in *History of Childhood Quarterly* 1:503-75, Spring 1974.

20. Ibid., pp. 507-08.

21. Ibid., p. 503.

22. Ibid., p. 554.

23. Ibid., p. 556.

24. Kern, Stephen. "Freud and the Discovery of Child Sexuality," *History of Childhood Quarterly* 1:117-41, Summer 1973; Saffady, William. "Fears of Sexual License During the English Reformation," *History of Childhood Quarterly* 1:89-97, Summer 1973; Trexler, Richard C. "Infanticide in Florence: New Sources and First Results," *History of Childhood Quarterly* 1:98-116, Summer 1973; Goodich, Michael. "Childhood and Adolescence Among the Thirteenth-Century Saints," *History of Childhood Quarterly* 1:285-309, Fall 1973; and Kern, Stephen.

"Explosive Intimacy: Psychodynamics of the Victorian Family," *History of Childhood Quarterly* 1:437-62, Winter 1974.

25. Beisel, David R. "Toward a Psychohistory of Jimmy Carter," *The Journal of Psychohistory* 1:201-38, Fall 1977.

26. Kett, Joseph F. "The Evolution of Childhood" (review), *American Historical Review.* 80:1296, Dec. 1975.

27. Shorter, Edward. *The Making of the Modern Family.* New York, Basic Books, 1975.

28. Ibid., pp. 3-8, 119, 203-04.

29. Lasch, Christopher. "What the Doctor Ordered," *New York Review of Books* 22:53, Dec. 11, 1975.

30. Stone, op. cit.

31. Ibid., pp. 653, 99.

32. Ibid., p. 174.

33. Kett, Joseph F. "The Evolution of Families and Emotions," *Chronicle of Higher Education* 15:15, Feb. 6, 1978.

34. Pletsch, Carl. "*The History of Childhood*" (review), *Journal of Modern History* 47:338, June 1975.

35. Macfarlane, Alan. "*The Family, Sex, and Marriage in England, 1500-1800*" (review), *History and Theory* 18:122, 1979.

36. Hobhouse, Christopher. *Fox.* London, John Murray, 1934, pp. 3-5.

37. Greven, Philip J. *The Protestant Temperament: Patterns of Child-Rearing, Religious Experience, and the Self in Early America.* New York, Knopf, 1977.

38. Ibid., p. 38.

39. Ibid., p. 151.

40. Ibid., p. 265.

41. Macfarlane, op. cit., p. 125.

42. Laslett, Peter. *Family Life and Illicit Love in Earlier Generations.* New York, Cambridge University Press, 1977, pp. 18-19.

43. Benton, John F. "The Evolution of Childhood" (review), *History of Childhood Quarterly* 1:588, Spring 1974.

APPENDIX

The History of Childhood: A Bibliography of
Selected Works by Historians

General

Ariès, Philippe. *Centuries of Childhood: A Social History of Family Life.* New York, Knopf, 1962. A widely cited study of the "invention" of the concept of childhood in France between the thirteenth and eighteenth centuries.

DeMause, Lloyd, ed. *The History of Childhood.* New York, Psychohistory Press, 1974. A collection of essays on childhood in different countries during different centuries introduced by a controversial essay by the editor in which he outlines stages of child rearing in world history.

Hunt, David. *Parents and Children in History.* New York, Basic Books, 1970. The book concentrates on seventeenth-century France, but it also discusses the contributions of Philippe Ariès and Erik Erikson to the study of the history of childhood.

Laslett, Peter, and Wall, Richard, eds. *Household and Family in Past Time.* Cambridge, Cambridge University Press, 1972. A series of essays on the size of households and levels of fertility by members of the Cambridge Group for the History of Population and Social Structure.

Lopes, Manuel D. "A Guide to the Interdisciplinary Literature of the History of Childhood," *History of Childhood Quarterly* 1:463-94, Winter 1974.

Rabb, Theodore K., and Rothberg, Robert I., eds. *The Family in History.* New York, Harper, 1973.

Rosenberg, Charles E., et al. *The Family in History.* Philadelphia, University of Pennsylvania Press, 1975. A variety of essays ranging in subject matter from sixteenth-century England to modern China and Dr. Spock.

Shorter, Edward. *The Making of the Modern Family.* New York, Basic Books, 1975. The author argues that "good mothering is an invention of modernization," and that infanticide and abandonment declined and husbands and wives became more affectionate during the later eighteenth and nineteenth centuries.

Stewart, Abigail J., et al. "Coding Categories for the Study of Child-Rearing from Historical Sources," *Journal of Interdisciplinary History* 5:687-701, Spring 1975.

Eighteenth- and Nineteenth-Century United States

Bremner, Robert H., ed. *Children and Youth in America: A Documentary History, 1600-1973.* Cambridge, Mass., Harvard University Press, 1970. A three-part collection (in five volumes) on the history of public policy toward children and youth, published under the auspices of the American Public Health Association with Robert Bremner, professor of history at Ohio State University, serving as executive research editor.

Calhoun, Arthur W. *A Social History of the American Family.* Cleveland, Arthur Clark Co., 1918. The classic early twentieth-century account.

Fleming, Sanford. *Children and Puritanism: The Place of Children in the Life and Thought of the New England Churches, 1620-1847* (Yale Studies in Religious Education, no. 8). New Haven, Conn., Yale University Press, 1933.

Greven, Philip. *Child-Rearing Concepts, 1628-1861: Historical Sources.* Itasca, Ill., F.E. Peacock, 1973.

_____ . *The Protestant Temperament: Patterns of Child-Rearing, Religious Experience, and the Self in Early America.* New York, Knopf, 1977. A thoughtful analysis of the implications of the overlapping "evangelical," "moderate," and "genteel" modes of child rearing.

Grotberg, Edith H., ed. *200 Years of Children.* Washington, D.C., USDHEW, Office of Human Development, 1977. A collection of bicentennial essays on health, education, child care, recreation, literature, and law by HEW specialists and others. The essays are not documented and are of mixed quality.

Handlin, Oscar, and Handlin, Mary F. *Facing Life: Youth and the Family in American History.* Boston, Little, Brown and Co., 1968. A popular survey of the subject of young men and women leaving home during the eighteenth, nineteenth, and twentieth centuries, as illustrated by brief biographies.

Kett, Joseph F. *Rites of Passage: Adolescence in America, 1790 to the Present.* New York, Basic Books, 1977. A survey of changing adult attitudes toward teenagers in the nineteenth and twentieth centuries.

Lasch, Christopher. *Haven in a Heartless World: The Family Besieged.* New York, Basic Books, 1977. The book argues that the nineteenth-century bourgeois family did a better job of bringing up children than its critics have conceded and that the twentieth-century "helping professions" have hurt the family more than they have helped the children.

Morgan, Edmund Sears. *Virginians at Home: Family Life in the Eighteenth Century.* Williamsburg, Va., Colonial Williamsburg, Inc., 1952. The evidence is necessarily more plentiful for the planters (and the slaves) than for other groups in the social scale. Separate chapters are devoted to children, courtship, and recreation.

Rapson, Richard C. "American Children as Seen by British Travelers, 1845-1935," *American Quarterly* 17:520, 1965.

Slater, Peter Gregg. *Children in the New England Mind.* Hamden, Conn., Shoe String Press, 1977. Four essays that appraise the implications of the seventeenth-century Puritan belief in the innate depravity of children and the substitution, by the early nineteenth century, of the romantic belief in the ineffable goodness of children.

Wishy, Bernard. *The Child and the Republic: The Dawn of Modern American Child Nurture.* Philadelphia, University of Pennsylvania Press, 1968. The book concentrates on religious ideals and moral indoctrination as drawn from the work of contemporary "experts" and supplemented by an analysis of children's stories. The first eight chapters deal with "The Child Redeemable" (1830-60), the last seven with "The Child Redeemed" (1860-1900).

Eighteenth- and Nineteenth-Century Britain

Anderson, Michael. *Family Structure in Nineteenth Century Lancashire.* Cambridge, Cambridge University Press, 1971. An evaluation of the impact of the industrial revolution on working-class family life.

Bayne-Powell, Rosamond. *The English Child in the Eighteenth Century.* London, J. Murray, 1939. A readable but unfootnoted survey drawn mostly from memoirs, with four chapters devoted to education and others to "Religion and the Child," "The Law and the Child," "The Child in Illness," etc.

Gathorne-Hardy, Jonathan. *The Rise and Fall of the British Nanny.* London, Hodder and Stoughton, 1972. A somewhat speculative survey of a phenomenon that crystallized during the first half of the nineteenth century and reached its heyday during the mid- and late Victorian years.

Hall, William C. *The Queen's Reign for Children.* London, T.F. Unwin, 1897. A Diamond Jubilee survey of how life had improved for children during Queen Victoria's reign.

Laslett, Peter. *Family Life and Illicit Love in Earlier Generations.* New York, Cambridge University Press, 1977. A collection of essays by best-known British demographic historians of our day on subjects like "Long-Term Trends in Bastardy" and "Age at Sexual Maturity." The first essay provides a theoretical overview of the English family before industrialization.

Lynd, Sylvia. *English Children.* London, W. Collins, 1942. A very brief illustrated survey of the lives of children from the Middle Ages to the twentieth century.

Pinchbeck, Ivy, and Hewitt, Margaret. *Children in English Society.* 2 vols. London, Routledge and Kegan Paul, 1969-73. The single most comprehensive survey of social and legal attitudes toward English children. Volume I carries the story to 1800, and Volume II to the mid-twentieth century, with special emphasis given to the increasing importance of the state in providing education and welfare service.

Stone, Lawrence. *The Family, Sex, and Marriage in England, 1500-1800.* New York, Harper & Row, 1977. Over 800 pages of information plus an underlying thesis, that of the move from the "open lineage family" of the sixteenth century that neglected children to the eighteenth-century family of "affective individualism" that coddled them. The evidence is necessarily drawn largely from aristocratic and gentry accounts.

Trumbach, Randolph. *The Rise of the Egalitarian Family: Aristocratic Kinship and Domestic Relations in Eighteenth-Century England.* New York, Academic Press, 1978. The study argues that in the course of the century the aristocratic family was transformed so that there was equality between man and wife and so that wives (and even husbands) spent far more time with their children. Trumbach does not attempt to explain this phenomenon, and his claim that the aristocracy served as a model to other ranks in society has been challenged.

Wohl, Anthony, ed. *The Victorian Family: Structure and Stresses.* New York, St. Martin's Press, 1978. A miscellany of essays on subjects ranging from patterns of childbirth, to working-class incest, to the Victorian paterfamilias, to Victoria's handling of children.

N—NARCISSE A TROUVÉ DES OISEAUX DANS UN NID.

O—OLIVIER, AVEC SON PARAPLUIE, N'A
PAS PEUR DE L'ORAGE.

The Maxine Waldron Collection of
Children's Books and Paper Toys

MARGARET N. COUGHLAN

The Waldron collection of childhood materials came to my attention while I was attempting to identify collections of historical children's books in a six-state geographic area for the National Planning for Special Collections Committee of ALA's Association for Library Service to Children. References in d'Alté Welch's bibliography[1] of American children's books to the holdings of the Henry Francis duPont Winterthur Museum in Delaware led me to write to Winterthur for information. I learned then that the museum's small but fine collection had been enriched in 1974 by Mrs. Maxine Waldron's gift of children's books and paper toys. Children's books, I was told, have always been of interest to the museum for their bindings, bookmaking and illustration, as well as for their reflection of social history.

I visited the museum libraries, spending two afternoons exploring Mrs. Waldron's nineteenth- and early twentieth-century children's materials—and, of course, taking a look at the museum's other rare children's books. Mrs. Neville Thompson, Mrs. James Taylor, and Mrs. Christine Edmondson were immensely helpful in seeing that I was able to get an idea of the riches in both areas.

On another occasion I visited Mrs. Waldron and spent some time leafing through her boxes and scrapbooks. She attributes her interest in these materials to a childhood love of paper dolls. She was an only child, she said, and grew up on a farm. One of her greatest delights at that time was the arrival of *Godey's Lady's Book,* for each issue contained a sheet of paper dolls and costumes. These dolls were her favorite toys, since money for such luxuries as purchased toys was scarce.

As a young woman she studied art at Teachers College of Columbia University in New York, and after graduation worked for two years on the staff of the Metropolitan Museum of Art's department of education. Before her marriage she taught art in various private schools around New York.

Art, fashion and interior decoration are her great interests. At one time she wanted to write and illustrate books for children. Instead, she said, she found herself collecting children's books, paper dolls, paper toys, and games, for she was fascinated by their reflection of popular taste in clothing, interior design, and amusements. She chose Winterthur as depository because of its concern with furniture, interior decoration, bookmaking, printing, and social history.

The Waldron collection is housed in two areas in the museum's libraries: almost 500 books are in the Rare Book Room of the Printed Book and Periodical Library, and over 18 boxes of paper dolls and toys are in the Downs Manuscript Collection. The collection contains some rarities: *Tales and Fables,* "selected by T. Ticklepitcher, from the works of eminent writers, both ancient and modern, for the improvement and instruction of the rising generation" (London, John Marshall, 1780?); an ornate dress of chenille and paper dating from the 1600s; and a "Protean Figure," issued April 1, 1811, by S. & J. Fuller of London at "the Temple of Fancy." This doll has twelve changes of costume, including those of a gentleman of 1700 in full attire, a monk, a knight in a suit of armor, and a Quaker.

Among nineteenth-century publishers whose books are represented is Samuel Wood, an earnest, religious gentleman who himself wrote most of the children's books he published—he considered those of the time unsuitable. Although his little volumes were not unattractive (they were illustrated with copperplate engravings both plain and hand-colored), they were heavily moralistic. It is recorded that Wood at first carried his books around with him in his pocket to give, as advertisement, to the children he encountered.[2]

The Babcocks of New Haven are also represented by a few publications. They, too, were not inspired publishers. As did many at the time, they obtained from England a number of children's books and "Americanized" them for a young audience. The titles sound beguiling; one of their toybooks, *The Snow Drop; A Collection of Nursery Rhymes,* could suggest to the unwary lightness and gaiety. However, it contains pieces with such titles as "For a Little Girl that Did Not Like to be Washed" and "About Learning to Read," along with, I am happy to say, the familiar "Twinkle, Twinkle, Little Star."

Works by well-known nineteenth- and twentieth-century illustrators are represented: the Dalziel Brothers, Kate Greenaway, Walter Crane, Randolph Caldecott, Palmer Cox, and Pamela Bianco. There are numerous editions of familiar nursery tales issued by minor firms and illustrated by unknown artists: *A Visit from St. Nicholas* and *In the Forest,* published by Louis Prang of Boston; *The Little Colonel's Doll Book;* books originating in France, Germany and England, many of them about dolls; pop-up books, including a *Cendrillon, ou la petite pantoufle de verre;* C. von Dichter's *Sechs bewegliche Bilder* ("moving figures in color," Vienna, 1882); and some Japanese books with English-language texts on paper-folding and dolls, all but three originating in Japan.

The collection contains 146 volumes published by the McLoughlin Brothers, nineteenth- to mid-twentieth-century predecessors of the Little Golden Books. These mass-produced books are important because they found their way into scores of homes across the country, influencing the taste and values of countless children. The range and quality of the firm's work is revealed in the Waldron holdings of books, games, paper dolls, and doll houses and furniture. Of particular interest, because they have copyright dates, are an 1856 *Little Red Riding Hood* and an 1869 *The Queen of Hearts and the Damson Tarts.* I need not point out that McLoughlins with copyright dates are not plentiful. Most of the Waldron collection titles were issued between 1875 and 1900, in such series as those "by" the ubiquitous, anonymous Aunt Jenny, Aunt Friendly, Uncle Ned, and Aunt Grumble; and by Little Pleasewell, Young America, and Little Slovenly Peter. With the possible exception of the fairy tales, individual titles in the collection—*Cross Child* and *Industrious Boy* (Young America), *Greedy Ben* (Little Pleasewell), and *Pauline and the Matches* (Peter Prim)—stress moral values and patriotism.

McLoughlin paper toys include "Wide World Costume Dolls," paper doll houses and furniture, booklets in the shape of dolls, nursery rhyme dolls, a *Model Book of Animals*, a Red Riding Hood game, and "The Round Game of Tiddly Winks."

The McLoughlin publications were enormously popular. In fact, their influence on children's works was so strong that a brief description of the firm is in order here. The following excerpt from John McLoughlin, Jr.'s obituary notice in *Publishers Weekly* (May 6, 1905) reveals the personality of this leading entrepreneur and the wide audience his firm's products reached:

> No obstacle ever arose in his path but it was in the end swept away. When he first took hold of the children's book and game business there was but little order or system in the business. The books were quaint but poorly printed and illustrated. The colors were laboriously put on by hand with stencils. Mr. McLoughlin introduced the then wonderful process of printing from relief [sic] etched zinc plates....From that time forward he led and others followed. Every child in the land knows the McLoughlin toys and books, and even across the seas their editions of "Mother Goose" has [sic] been sent printed in many languages. In fact, the history in the last decade of colored toy books for youngsters is the history of Mr. McLoughlin and his firm.

Although the firm's products were widely distributed, until recently relatively little has been known about the publishing firm itself. John Tebbel, in his substantial, now three-volume history of American publishing, records that it was begun in 1828 by a Scottish coachmaker and carpenter, John McLoughlin, who came to this country in 1819. He found his way into printing through a friendship with Robert Hoe, a maker of wooden printing presses and type. McLoughlin studied printing and worked for a short time for the New York *Times*. When that paper ceased publishing a year later, he went into business for himself, with a second-hand press and some type, and began to write and publish moralistic tracts and leaflets for the young. These were issued separately at first, and then later collected between covers as McLoughlin's Books for Children. About 1840, the firm merged with that of a competitor, John Elton, and became John Elton & Company.

The future genius behind the firm, John McLoughlin, Jr., entered the concern while still a boy, and as a young man he became a partner. Upon the retirements of his father and John Elton, he took control of the firm under his own name. In the 1850s, he brought his younger brother Edmund into the business as a partner, and McLoughlin Brothers was born. Young John was an innovator and among the first in the United States to print from zinc plates of his own making produced by the photoengraving process. The firm began issuing toy books, the first to be printed in color in America. These were so successful that the firm soon did nothing else. For many years its only competition came from English imports.

Some of the best artists of the century worked for the firm: Thomas Nast, the well-known political cartoonist for *Harper's Weekly*, whose *Yankee Doodle* sold well into the twentieth century; G.A. Davis, "the Jessie Willcox Smith of her time"; Helena A. Maguire, an English painter of animals; Palmer Cox of "Brownie" fame; Howard Pyle; Harrison Cady, a long-time contributor to *St. Nicholas* magazine as well as illustrator of many of Thornton Burgess's works; and Gordon Grant, noted for his drawings of ships and sailors. It is reported that the demand for the firm's products was so great that it had at one time a staff of seventy-five artists designing books, games and paper dolls.[3]

After the death of John McLoughlin, Jr., the business was conducted by his sons. They, however, lacked their father's interest in the business, and sold it in 1920 to the Milton Bradley Company, which continued it as a subsidiary under its old name. New leadership, that of Edward O. Clark and his son Edward, Jr., restored the firm's fortunes, and it did well in the thirties and forties. However, World War II ended its prosperity; it fell into the hands of bankers, was sold to a toy manufacturer (Julius Kushner, of Kushner & Jacobs), and by 1970 ceased to exist.

Among novelty items in the Waldron holdings of interest to collectors are toy books with paper doll characters issued by S. & J. Fuller of London. The Waldron collection also includes *The History and Adventures of Little Henry* (11th ed., London, 1830) and *The History of Little Fanny* (3d ed., London, 1810). Each is "exemplified" in a series of figures with which a child, after cutting out the figures, hats and heads, could dramatize the story. Since the plots are similar, I shall describe here only that of *Little Fanny*.

Too fond of play, idle, and vain, Fanny falls from riches to rags, and after hard work and repentance is reconciled with her loving mama. The book concludes:

> Once more the little Fanny you must see,
> Since she's returned to what she ought to be;
> She's now no longer idle, proud, or vain,
> Eager her own opinion to maintain,
> But pius, modest, dilligent, and mild,
> Belov'd by all, a good and happy child.

Movable and pop-up books, issued by three well-known English firms, Tuck, Nister, and Dean; paper dolls and costumes; valentines and Christmas cards are well represented in the Waldron holdings. The collection contains also a model village and dairy yard, peep shows,

panoramas, and Pollock's Toy Theatre, complete with characters, scenes, and booklet for the *Forty Thieves*. Another stage set, for *Lord Darnley*, is incomplete. There is a "Webb's Juvenile Drama," accompanied by a booklet which tells in sixteen scenes the story of the battles of Balaklava and Inkerman. And there are picture sheets, paper dolls and soldiers, and *pantins* (cardboard human figures with jointed neck, body, and limbs) issued by Épinal, a French firm famous for its *Imagerie populaire*. Items from Germany include turn-of-the-century *pantins*, paper fashion dolls, and two sheets of *figuren* for a *kindertheater*. There are, too, assorted games and a stereopticon with original plates.

The importance of the Waldron collection for the scholar is that it constitutes primary source material for study of the mass-produced book, the history of fashion, popular taste in interior decoration and home amusements, as well as for study of printing, illustration and bookmaking.

References

1. Welch, d'Alté A. *A Bibliography of American Children's Books Printed Prior to 1821.* Worcester, Mass., American Antiquarian Society and Barre Publishers, 1972.

2. Tebbel, John W. *A History of Book Publishing in the United States.* New York, Bowker, 1972, vol. 1, p. 327.

3. Ibid., vol 3 (1978), p. 270.

P—PAULINE A BEAUCOUP DE PLAISIR AVEC
  SA PETITE POUPÉE.

Q—QUENTIN AIME À JOUER AUX QUILLES
DE BOIS.

Lydia Maria Child and the
Juvenile Miscellany

CAROLYN L. KARCHER

L ydia Maria Child has yet to inspire a biography worthy of her
leading role in prodding the conscience of antebellum America,
as an antislavery propagandist and as a children's writer.[1] These
dual aspects of her career meet in the pages of the *Juvenile Miscellany*,
the children's periodical she founded in 1826 and edited until its collapse
in 1834. Yet the meeting is a problematic one. As a children's writer,
Child embraced the mission of diffusing the morality of the rising middle
class among the widest possible audience, thus making it the means of
bridging class conflicts in a society where they were beginning to break
into the open. As an abolitionist, on the contrary, Child necessarily
assumed the burden of stirring controversy on a bitterly divisive issue
which the majority of her middle- and upper-class readers wanted at all
costs to keep under a lid. The basic incompatibility of the two aims Child
struggled to fuse in her children's magazine is evident both in other

children's writers' gingerly handling of the slavery issue[2] and in the fate that befell the *Juvenile Miscellany* once Child openly challenged her readers' prejudices in her famous abolitionist tract of 1833, *An Appeal in Favor of That Class of Americans Called Africans.* For a few brief years, however, Child succeeded remarkably well in incorporating a radical critique of slavery and racism into a vehicle for transmitting the dominant class's value system to its children and their future subordinates. The strategies she adopted to reconcile her roles as a mouthpiece of bourgeois morality on the one hand and of unpopular antislavery doctrine on the other are the subject of this paper.

The question to be asked at the outset is, what impelled Child to undertake the responsibility of socializing children? One answer, perhaps, arises out of her own life. Writing for children may have been a way of compensating for a motherless childhood and a childless adulthood— of vicariously satisfying a need to mother and be mothered. The upbringing of Lydia Maria Francis differed considerably from the ideal depicted in the stories and didactic dialogues of the *Juvenile Miscellany,* where young girls receive loving discipline from mothers who insist on proper grooming, regular tasks, and fixed hours of study. Instead, Maria lost her mother at age twelve. Her father, burying his grief in work, let Maria run wild in clothes whose shabbiness and slovenliness scandalized the neighbors.[3] Meanwhile, Maria experienced the added trauma, shared by so many nineteenth-century feminists, of seeing her brother go off to pursue his schooling at Harvard, leaving her to the makeshift instruction of a young ladies' seminary and such edification as she could snatch from the books in her father's library. Even this haphazard education was soon curtailed when her father decided to cure Maria of bookishness by sending her to live with her married sister in Maine.

Yet Maria's unschooled girlhood taught her two lessons more valuable than any her brother Convers learned at Harvard. When eight years old, Maria witnessed her father's rescue of a fugitive slave.[4] And later in Maine, Maria encountered remnants of the Penobscot Indian tribe and observed firsthand both the poverty to which the Indians had been reduced by white depredations and the dignity, "poetic fancy," artistry, and communal solidarity they nonetheless retained.[5] Out of this early exposure to the victimization of America's nonwhite races grew Lydia Maria Child's lifelong commitment to demanding justice for the Negro and the Indian. In turn, the formative influence of such youthful lessons suggests another reason why Child attached so much importance to firing children, as well as adults, with her ideal of human brotherhood: she must have realized that it is easier to prevent racial prejudice from taking root in young minds than to extirpate it in older ones.

When Child began editing the *Juvenile Miscellany* at the invitation of a Boston publishing firm, she had already made a name for herself as the author of two historical novels: *Hobomok* (1824), a romance introducing the daring theme of miscegenation between white woman and Indian, and *The Rebels* (1825), a tale of the American Revolution.[6] The magazine—one of the first devoted to the "instruction and amusement of youth," as its motto proclaimed—was an instant success. A half-century after its demise, a writer for the Unitarian Review fondly recalled how children had "sat on the stone steps of their house doors all the way up and down Chestnut Street in Boston, waiting for the carrier" to deliver the latest bimonthly issue of the *Juvenile Miscellany*. "Never did any one cater so wisely and so well for the unfolding mind," judged this late nineteenth-century eulogist. "The mere names of some of the stories... bring vivid pictures of past delight before us....In simplicity, directness, and moral influence, [the *Juvenile Miscellany*] remains superior to any of the illustrated magazines of to-day."[7] Further testifying to the extraordinary popularity the *Miscellany* enjoyed was the number of selections that rival children's magazines reprinted from it—sometimes without acknowledgment—both during its heyday and in later decades.[8]

The "Address to the Young" prefacing the first issue of the *Juvenile Miscellany* sets its tone and announces its dominant objectives:

> I seldom meet a little girl, even in the crowded streets of Boston, without thinking with anxious tenderness, concerning her education, her temper and her principles. Yes, *principles!* Children can act from good principle, as well as gentlemen and ladies....
> If I am able to convince you, that you *can* do whatever you *try* to do, in the acquisition of learning; if I can lead you to examine your own hearts and pray to your Heavenly Father to remove from thence whatsoever is evil, I shall be very happy....If you will *persevere;* if you will be *attentive;* if you will learn to *think for yourselves;* you can overcome all obstacles in the path of knowledge; and if you really *wish* to be good, there is a kind Parent, in the heavens, who will help you in every endeavor you make, to be virtuous and religious.[9]

The themes, to be sure, are common to all antebellum children's writers, as Anne MacLeod has shown in her fine monograph on children's fiction and nineteenth-century American culture.[10] Yet the words about acquiring learning, thinking for oneself, and relying on "a kind Parent" in heaven resonate with a special poignancy when one thinks of Child's early hunger for education and parental care.

The *Juvenile Miscellany* lives up to its inaugural address. Directly or indirectly, almost every selection in the magazine aims to inculcate in its young readers the "principles" that would enable them to become virtuous and useful members of nineteenth-century American society—

principles that would also, as Child believed, help them resolve the tensions between city and country, rich and poor, white and nonwhite that threatened American society's cohesiveness. Let us, then, begin our review of the *Juvenile Miscellany* by enumerating these principles, before proceeding to focus on how Child applied them to social issues, and particularly to the issue she tackled most courageously: slavery.

The virtues the *Juvenile Miscellany* preaches are those of the Protestant ethic: industry, time-consciousness, perseverance, attentiveness, orderliness, self-control, obedience, honesty, self-denial, and charity. With the exception of charity, these virtues serve primarily to make productive workers out of both the rising entrepreneurial class and the laboring class it rules. Secondarily—and this is where charity comes in—they serve to temper the competitiveness, selfishness, and individualism inherent in bourgeois society[11] and to foster harmony and goodwill among its contending members—an end to which the single standard of austere behavior for rich and poor alike leads.

A New Year's message to children, entitled "Value of Time," explicitly voices the economic impulse behind the glorification of routine. "Time is money," it reminds children, in the words of that bourgeois patron saint, Benjamin Franklin. "Time is learning, too. That is, a diligent use of it, will procure both wealth and knowledge." Hence children ought to "make a regular arrangement" of their time and strive to be "always employed."[12] Similarly, the tale "The French Orphan, or... The New Year's Reward" dramatizes the material benefits of another Protestant virtue, honesty. The heroine of this tale resists the temptation to appropriate a gold medallion apparently dropped by one of her mother's rich pupils. Were she to pawn or sell the medallion, she would be able to buy medicine for her mother and sister, who are desperately ill. Instead, the girl returns the medallion to its owner. Although her mother and sister die soon afterward, her reward is to be succored by the rich family to whom the medallion belongs, and to be greeted at the end of the story with the miraculous reappearance of her long-lost father, who has made a fortune in the interim.[13]

The function of charity in forestalling class conflict, hinted at in "The French Orphan," is uppermost in a fascinating tale that shows class divisions in the making: "The Cottage Girl." The story opens with the death of a poverty-sticken workingwoman and the adoption of her orphaned twins, a boy and a girl, by a kindly washerwoman who is almost as poor herself. In remarking on the contrast between the charity this poor washerwoman displays and the heartlessness the rich seem to evince, Child, like Elizabeth Gaskell in England, supposes that the rich are simply unaware of poverty and she sees it as her mission to enlighten them. "A great many people in Boston would have helped" this needy family, and "a great many happy little girls and boys...would have felt willing to part with their choicest playthings" to do so, Child insists, if only "they had known of their distress."[14]

Shortly after the children's adoption, a client of the washerwoman offers to bring up the little boy, and poverty compels the washerwoman to agree, despite her reluctance to separate the children. The boy and his new foster mother move to another part of Massachusetts, where she eventually remarries and confides him to the care of a wealthy family. Some years later, by one of those coincidences dear to nineteenth-century romancers, the wealthy family settles in Boston, right next door to the poor washerwoman and her adopted daughter. By this time the two children, who have long since lost touch, have all but forgotten each other, and when they meet, the social disparity between them at first prevents them from recognizing each other. The recognition is attended by awkwardness on both sides. The sister suddenly becomes conscious of her shabby clothes and unrefined manners, and the brother experiences a conflict between fraternal and class loyalties.

The boy's foster parents share his misgivings about his sister: "They were a little afraid they should find her a vulgar, ignorant, and impudent girl, because she had had no chance for education."[15] Although they are agreeably surprised by the girl's "natural politeness," reflecting an upbringing that has "educated her *heart*" if not her mind, everyone is relieved when she elects to show her gratitude to the washerwoman by remaining with her, rather than to accept the rich family's offer of adoption.

With class lines thus preserved, the two families establish what Child apparently regards as the ideal relationship between rich and poor, the rich family providing money to send the girl "to a good school" and frequently making her "presents of neat, suitable clothing" (suitable to her station in life, that is), the poor family reciprocating with gratitude and sober conduct. This relationship persists after the children grow up. The girl marries a "sensible, industrious man, who owned a good farm in Connecticut." Her brother, now a "prosperous" manufacturer, continues to send her "many a handsome present" and to eat Thanksgiving dinner at her "plain, but plentiful table" every year. Thus a story that begins with urban poverty threatening the cohesion of the family ends with class literally dividing twin brother from sister (in according the male sibling the higher status, was Child commenting on women's subordination?), and resolves the social contradictions by invoking private charity and fantasizing a return to rural origins.

To point out the ideological connotations of the morality Child preaches in the *Juvenile Miscellany* is by no means to accuse her of hypocrisy or cynicism, however. Child believed fervently in the principles she taught, and her own life was a model of the self-sacrifice that the conscientious fulfillment of moral duty entailed. It was also a model of the contradictions her society's creed contained. For Child found herself transformed from a voice of social conservatism into an agent of radicalism as soon as she applied her ideal of charity to Indians and blacks. It was still possible, in the 1820s, to view poverty as a problem that could be alleviated case by case, through private charity, without calling into question the premises on which American society was based. It was not possible to view the dispossession and extermination of the Indians and the enslavement of blacks in these terms.

Thus in contrast to her tales, sketches, and didactic dialogues about white children, which reinforce American bourgeois values and exalt the heroes who personify them, like Benjamin Franklin and George Washington, Child's writings about Indians and blacks subvert the culture's dominant myths and dethrone its heroes. In vindicating the Indians, for example, Child quite consciously seeks—as she spells out in the preface to her 1829 tract, *The First Settlers of New-England: or, Conquest of the Pequods, Narragansets and Pokanokets: As Related by a Mother to Her Children, and Designed for the Instruction of Youth*[16]—to dispel the "general misapprehension" regarding Indian conduct and character. This means challenging the Puritan chroniclers of Indian wars, exposing their bigotry, and rewriting colonial history from the Indians' point of view to emphasize the kindness Indians showed whites and the unprovoked persecution with which it was requited. Child's purpose in *The First Settlers of New-England*, moreover, is not merely to indulge in breastbeating for past crimes against the Indians, but to spur her readers to act against the new crimes then being committed by the federal government under Andrew Jackson: the hounding of the Seminoles in Florida and the expulsion of the Cherokees from Georgia.[17]

Although Child's rhetoric is more muted in the *Juvenile Miscellany*, her strategy of promoting sympathy for the Indians is the same, and her concern for their plight—which engaged her attention almost until the end of her literary career, eliciting her *Appeal for the Indians* in 1868—is no less apparent. Indeed, the story heading the very first number of the *Miscellany* introduces the issue of Indian-white relations and shows the first settlers living in harmony with the Indians. At the beginning of the story, a "poor sick Indian woman, unable to follow her tribe" in the hunt, appears at the door of a Puritan settler begging for food. The settler's wife responds generously and reaps her reward a year later, when the Indian woman finds the couple's childen wandering in the woods and brings them safely home. Had the early settlers continued to treat the Indians in this fraternal spirit, the story implies, a permanent symbiotic relationship might have prevailed between the races and the tragic sequel of race war been averted.[18]

Child offers her version of that sequel in a later number of the *Miscellany*. Two of the dialogues between aunt and nephew in the series entitled "American History" deal with the Pequod and King Philip's Wars.[19] Dating from the same period as *The First Settlers of New-England*, but apparently addressed to an audience whose prejudices were more virulent (if the views ascribed to the nephew are any indication), these dialogues attempt to dispute the popular stereotype of Indians as malign savages who massacred helpless whites without any motive. "We must not blame them too much," the aunt in the dialogue reproves her nephew, when he expresses the usual revulsion against Indian cruelty. "They had suffered much from the injustice and thoughtlessness of some of the white settlers....Besides, they foresaw that if the English settlements were allowed to increase, their hunting grounds would be taken from them, and their tribes cease to exist." Unlike *The First Settlers*, the *Juvenile Miscellany* dialogues do not specify the acts of white aggression that sparked the Pequod and King Philip's Wars, but they do once again drive home the contemporary relevance of the sorry history they recount: "Even to this day, some white men talk and act as if they thought Indians were brutes, destitute of reason and of feeling; and since Indians have as much reason and feeling as we have, it is not strange that they deeply resent such treatment."[20]

The attitude Child herself reveals toward Indians in the sketches based on her visits to their Maine camps is often patronizing. Yet she also shows genuine respect for the Indians' communal values, even when they clash with the bourgeois creed of private poverty to which she subscribes. For example, immediately after reporting that the Indians "cannot be made to believe that the woods belong to one man more than another," she allows them to expound their own philosophy of property in reply to remonstrances against cutting down trees on privately owned land: "You have wood enough to burn—what for you want more wood? When you die, you no carry wood with you."[21]

None of the *Miscellany*'s stories about Indians propose any specific measures for redressing Indian wrongs—in this respect the *Miscellany* is certainly more reticent than *The First Settlers*. Nevertheless, insofar as they attack the racial stereotypes used to justify the dispossession and extermination of the Indians, they call into question the structural basis of American society, as none of Child's stories about the white poor do. The radical implications of championing America's nonwhite victims become even more apparent in the thirteen *Miscellany* selections that deal with slavery and anti-Negro prejudice.[22]

The *Juvenile Miscellany* gives more extensive coverage to these controversial issues than any other contemporary children's periodical.[23] Yet because Child opts for an indirect mode of preaching against slavery, and because she concentrates on combating Northern racial prejudice, rather than on denouncing Southern cruelty, historians of children's literature have represented her as soft-pedaling her criticism of slavery in the *Miscellany*.[24] This view, I believe, derives from a misreading of Child's abolitionist writings for adults, and from a failure to appreciate the degree to which the issue of racial prejudice dominates them, too. Thus in order to understand Child's handling of slavery in the *Juvenile Miscellany*, we must begin by taking a closer look at her *Appeal in Favor of That Class of Americans Called Africans*, which she was planning and writing over the last years of the *Miscellany*'s existence, approximately from 1830 to 1833.

Compared to the writings of her mentor Garrison, Child's *Appeal* is a model of rhetorical tact. Its very title is disarming. The preface with which it opens "beseech[es]" the reader "not to throw down this volume as soon as you have glanced at the title," but to "read it, on any terms": "for an hour's amusement to yourself, or benefit to your children," for a "fresh occasion to sneer at the vulgarity of the cause," for "sheer curiosity to see what a woman (who had much better attend to her household concerns) will say upon such a subject."[25] We should pay special heed to those words "benefit to your children," for they tell us how urgently Child felt the need to extend her antislavery message to children.

Not only does the *Appeal* eschew the invective tone of Garrison's *The Liberator* but, unlike Harriet Martineau's *Society in America* (1837) and Theodore Weld's *American Slavery As It Is* (1839), it devotes relatively little space to exposing and condemning the brutality of Southern slavery per se. Even where it anatomizes the "Inevitable Effect" of slavery "upon All Concerned in It" (the title of the first chapter), the *Appeal* does so by taking a "Comparative View of Slavery, in Different Ages and Nations" (the title of the second). This strategy, while sometimes revealing Southern slave law as more oppressive than that of other slave societies, nevertheless treats Southerners as the heirs of a long tradition, and thus directs censure away from them and toward the institution of slavery itself. At the same time, this strategy permits an opportunity to examine precedents for emancipating slaves and integrating them into free society. The feasibility of such a solution to the slavery problem, in fact, is the chief subject of the *Appeal* and explains the feature that makes it so distinctive among abolitionist tracts: its concerted attempt to undermine the premise of black inferiority and savagery on which both the defense of slavery and the opposition to abolition rested. Three of the *Appeal*'s eight chapters vindicate the "Intellect" and "Moral Character of Negroes" and discuss "Prejudices against People of Color, and Our Duties in Relation to This Subject." The last of these, with which the *Appeal* concludes, addresses itself specifically to Child's fellow Northerners, whom it charges with harboring "prejudice against colored people....even more inveterate" than that of Southerners, and whom it calls upon to repeal their own segregation laws and prohibitions against racial intermarriage.[26]

How does the *Juvenile Miscellany* reflect the rhetorical strategy and message of the *Appeal*? First of all, it, too, seeks to disarm readers who might be inclined to "throw down this volume as soon as [they] have glanced at the title." Thus neither the title nor the format of a story like "William Peterson, the Brave and Good Boy," gives the reader any cause for rejecting its message out of hand. In eulogizing a boy for giving his life to rescue children who had fallen into a hole in the ice while skating, this moral tale follows all the conventions of its genre. Only at the end does Child reveal that "William Peterson was a colored boy," and the skaters he saved "all white boys." By then she can safely, and all the more effectively, spell out the lesson of "this *true* anecdote": "I believe no generous-minded white children, will be tempted to speak unkindly, or uncivilly, to people whom God has made of a color different from their own."[27]

Child circumvents parental censors in many other selections of the *Miscellany* by slipping antislavery commentary into unlikely places. In the midst of a review of arithmetic books, for example, Child introduces some testimony which the British abolitionist Thomas Clarkson had collected of African "mental dexterity...in arithmetic." "The Africans reckon *in their heads*," she quotes Clarkson as reporting, and perform "long and complicated" calculations with a "despatch and accuracy, surpassing...the European method" of reckoning on paper. After pointing out that this fact contradicts the popular assessment of the African intellect, she gently admonishes her "good little readers" that "it is very rash, and must be very offensive in the sight of God, whose children we all are, for any portion of the human family to arrogate to themselves a superiority over others."[28]

Similarly, Child interpolates into a long and otherwise innocuous article on dogs a graphic account of how the bloodhounds formerly used to capture runaway slaves in Santo Domingo (and still used for that purpose in the antebellum South, although Child does not say so) were trained "to this inhuman pursuit" by being kept on short rations while effigies of blacks, "stuffed with blood and entrails," were dangled in front of them.[29]

Just as beguilingly, articles with the innocent titles "Some Talk about Cuba" and "Some Talk about Brazil" (which begin like the other geography lessons in which the *Juvenile Miscellany* abounds) conclude by moralizing that these tropical paradises are flawed by "the greatest evil that can exist in any country"—slavery.[30] The analogy with the United States, often pictured by abolitionists as a fallen Eden, is obvious. But by leaving it unstated, Child is able to avoid fanning the flames of sectional strife, while freely expressing both her indignation at how slaves are "starved to death, and whipped to death" and her sympathy for the "despair and rage" that often lead them to "murder their masters and kill themselves."[31]

Besides reflecting the rhetorical tact of the *Appeal*, these articles on African mental dexterity and on slavery in Santo Domingo, Cuba and Brazil illustrate its second major strategy—that of bringing a comparative historical and cultural perspective to bear on the related questions of how slaves were treated and whether they were fit for freedom. Indeed, so closely does the *Miscellany* parallel the *Appeal* in its approach to these questions that it cites the same sources and sometimes even repeats the same arguments verbatim.[32]

At the heart of both the *Appeal* and the *Miscellany* is the attempt to combat the prejudices toward blacks that made abolition seem so unthinkable, even to Northern readers with no financial stake in slavery. Whereas the *Appeal* relies primarily on facts, logic and exhortation, however, the *Miscellany* often exploits the potentially more subversive means fiction affords of challenging the premises of slavery and racism. In different ways, the stories "The St. Domingo Orphans," "Jumbo and Zairee," and "Mary French and Susan Easton" all undermine racial stereotypes and dramatize the implications of slavery for the society that sanctions it.

The earliest of these, "The St. Domingo Orphans" (1830), dates from the period when Child was just beginning the extensive research on slavery that would culminate in the *Appeal* three years later.[33] Although the story conforms to stereotype in depicting the slave rebels as bloodthirsty savages (apparently Child had not yet revised her interpretation of the Santo Domingo tragedy), it counterbalances this view of the Negro by portraying several compassionate blacks, who help the beleaguered whites to escape. And the sequel altogether reverses the traditional stereotypes of black and white, exposing color as a highly unreliable indication of moral worth, and even of racial identity. On the one hand the widow of the rebel leader Dessalines demonstrates, by saving the orphaned daughters of a white planter from death, that "her heart was white, though her face was black." On the other hand, the white woman to whom she entrusts the orphans betrays them, and thus evinces "a black heart" despite her "white face."[34] Most subversively of all, the orphans fall prey to this woman because "exposure to a West-Indian sun had made them so dark, that they were easily mistaken for mulattoes," notwithstanding their white parentage.[35] In short, Child implies that the racial distinctions on which black slavery was based are so treacherous that they can as readily lead to the enslavement of "whites" as of "blacks." It is an insight that no other children's writer—and few abolitionists— achieved. The final ironic twist is that the orphans find themselves rescued from Santo Domingo, where slavery has been overthrown, only to be enslaved in the United States, where slavery continues to make a mockery out of libertarian ideals. Not until recognized one day by the French consul in Baltimore, a former friend of their mother's, do they regain their freedom—upon which they hasten to take refuge in France from American slavery. The note on which the story ends reiterates the message that the orphans have received better treatment at the hands of blacks—even in the throes of the bloodiest slave revolt in history—than at the hands of their own peers. They always speak of the blacks to whom they owe their lives with "tears of gratitude," reports Child, and "they never allow a ship to sail to St. Domingo" without sending their benefactors "some token of affectionate remembrance."[36]

Child's next antislavery story, "Jumbo and Zairee" (1831), has been singled out by historians of children's literature as the "most outspoken indictment of slavery" that she published in the *Juvenile Miscellany*.[37] What makes the story particularly interesting is its reworking of a historical incident originally written up in the *African Repository*, the organ of the Colonization Society, and subsequently reprinted in the *Youth's Companion*, the *Miscellany*'s chief rival among children's magazines.[38] A comparison of the three accounts of "Abduhl Rahhahman, the Unfortunate Moorish Prince," not only helps to situate Child vis-à-vis both the Colonization Society and other children's writers, but also sheds much light on her fictional strategies.

The historical figure whose case had come to the Colonization Society's attention was a Moorish prince of Timbuktu (the *Repository* makes much of the superiority to the Negro that Moorish ancestry confers on the prince).[39] The prince's family had once sheltered an American doctor and nursed him during a "long and painful illness." Later, in a campaign against a neighboring tribe, the prince had been captured by his enemies and sold to slave traders, by which means he had landed in Natchez, Mississippi. After a number of years in slavery, he encountered the American doctor his family had long ago befriended. The doctor sought unavailingly to purchase and emancipate the prince, in gratitude for past hospitality, but the prince's owner refused to relinquish him until old age diminished his utility. (The *Repository* glosses over this, though it is quite obvious from reading between the lines.) At the end of his life, the prince was finally being sent back to Africa by the Colonization Society, along with his wife and as many of his children as subscribers could raise money to redeem.

In contrast to the *Repository*, with its self-congratulatory emphasis on white benevolence, the *Youth's Companion* editorializes: "Abduhl Rahhahman is not the only African, who has claims upon our sympathies.—There are at this moment many hundreds of thousands of Africans in our country who are slaves to white men, and have no prospect for becoming free. There may not be any among them who were *princes* in Africa; but they are all *human beings*, who were torn from their country, from their homes, from their parents and neighbors and friends and sold into cruel bondage." Yet the *Companion* goes on to lament that "strange as it must seem,...mercy to the colored people themselves requires, that they should *for the present* continue as they are," since most of them are "unfit to take care of themselves and their families."[40]

In recasting the story of Abduhl Rahhahman, Child made a number of significant changes. First, she specifically adapted it to a juvenile audience by introducing the two children, Jumbo and Zairee, and centering the story on their experience, instead of on the prince's. Second, she identified the children as Africans, rather than as Moors, thus eliminating the racist implication that a Moor had higher claims on white sympathies. Third, she made Jumbo and Zairee the victims not of an enemy tribe, but of American slavers—a modification that allowed her to castigate the hypocrisy of those who enslaved their fellow beings while boasting of American freedom and equality.[41] Among her most radical changes, however, were to contrast African kindness toward whites with white perfidy toward Africans, and to allow her African characters to articulate their outrage at the ingratitude with which their generosity is requited.

For example, in describing the hospitality that the royal father of Jumbo and Zairee extends to the shipwrecked Englishman Mr. Harris, Child comments: "the English king could not have treated a guest with more kindness and generosity." Later, after Jumbo and Zairee have been captured by slavers upon going down to the beach to see off their father's guest, Child has their distraught mother exclaim: "She had rather, a thousand times over, that they had been swallowed by crocodiles, than to be carried off and made slaves by the white men. She hated the sound of a white man's name." To sharpen the sting, Child lets both parents suspect that their English guest has been responsible for kidnaping their children, with the result that the mother bans any mention of Mr. Harris in her hearing and the prince swears eternal vengeance against all white men.[42]

The theme of white ingratitude and the vengefulness it inspires becomes more prominent than ever when the prince himself is transported to Virginia as a slave and there discovers that his erstwhile protégé, Mr. Harris, has bought a plantation and become a slaveowner. Upon seeing "the white man, whom I had treated with so much kindness in my own country," says the prince, his blood boils, and he looks for an opportunity to kill his supposed betrayer. As it turns out, however, Mr. Harris greets the prince as a long-lost friend and determines to repay his debt to his African benefactor by buying him and his new-found children and sending them all back to Africa. He also concludes—and this is by far the most important interpolation Child made in her source—that slavery is "wrong in the sight of God." The upshot is that he frees all his slaves, sending them to Africa, too. Henceforth, the Africans remember him as "the good white man"—an exception among the race they have justly learned to hate.[43] The repatriation to Africa that accompanies emancipation may indicate that in 1831, Child still subscribed to the solution conservatives advocated to the slavery problem: gradual emancipation and colonization of the ex-slaves in Africa. Nevertheless, by suggesting that the only means of redeeming the Anglo-American image in African eyes is to emancipate the slaves forthwith and en masse, the story unmistakably points toward the radical doctrine of abolition, which she would advance in the *Appeal*.[44]

Perhaps the most moving of Child's antislavery stories, and certainly her most telling attack on racial prejudice in the *Juvenile Miscellany*, is "Mary French and Susan Easton," which appeared in the penultimate issue (May 1834).[45] Like "The St. Domingo Orphans," this tale seeks to illustrate the treacherousness of color as the basis for consigning some to slavery and others to freedom. The title characters are two little girls, one white and the other black, who have grown up together on the western shores of the Mississippi, across the river from slave territory. Both have been born free, but Susan's father was once a slave, having won his freedom by saving his master from a rattlesnake. Ironically, he himself falls victim to a metaphorical rattlesnake—a white slave-trader. One day as Mary and Susan are playing, a peddler turns up and entices them with his wares. On the pretext of taking them home to their parents to ask for money to buy something, he kidnaps them and takes them into the forest, where he cuts and frizzes Mary's hair and darkens her skin with a mixture of soot and grease. Then he sells the two girls to separate owners.

Mary, of course, attempts to win her release by claiming that she is white, but at first no one believes her. Only when she succeeds in washing off the soot and grease does she convince her owner that she has been illegally enslaved. At this point, Mary tries to enlist help in finding and freeing Susan, too, since she cannot "understand what right they had to take honest Paul Easton's daughter, and make her a slave, any more than they had to make a slave of *her* father's daughter." The answer, she is told, is that Susan is a "nigger," and that "*niggers* are used to being slaves." In vain does Mary plead that Susan, having been born free, is no more used to slavery than she, Mary, is. As a "nigger," Susan stands condemned to her fate. The story ends with contrasting tableaux. Mary is restored to her parents, who greet her with tears of joy. Susan's parents never recover their daughter; the tears they shed are tears of sorrow. Comments Child: "[Susan] is no doubt a slave, compelled to labor without receiving any wages for her hard work, and whipped whenever she dares to say that she has a right to be free." The final sentence trenchantly sums up the moral of the tale: "The only difference between Mary French and Susan Easton is, that the black color could be rubbed off from Mary's skin, while from Susan's it could not."[46]

"Mary French and Susan Easton" was the last significant piece of antislavery protest that Child contributed to the *Juvenile Miscellany*. Two months later, mass cancellation of subscriptions forced her to close down the magazine and to "bid a reluctant and most affectionate farewell to my little readers."[47] Ironically, the adult public that for three years had been quietly reading Child's admonitions against racial prejudice in the *Miscellany* reacted virulently against the same message when openly preached in her abolitionist manifesto, the *Appeal in Favor of That Class of Americans Called Africans*. This paradox raises some interesting questions: Why did it take the *Appeal* to show the public Child's true colors? Had her readers simply missed the point of sketches like "Some Talk about Brazil" and stories like "The St. Domingo Orphans" and "Mary French and Susan Easton," or were they recoiling from overt agitation of a divisive issue? More fundamentally, did Child succeed better at converting readers to abolitionism by subtly undermining their prejudices in a neutral forum—at the risk of having her message escape readers—or by boldly denouncing slavery and racism in polemical tracts—at the risk of alienating the majority, while winning over a minority? Unfortunately, there is no way of answering such questions without testimony from juvenile readers as to the impact that the *Miscellany*'s antislavery stories had on them later in life.

One thing is certain, however. The collapse of the *Juvenile Miscellany* marked the end of Child's vain attempt to reconcile her conflicting roles as a custodian of traditional values and as an agent of their overthrow. For the following decade, she devoted herself primarily to abolitionism; and in the years to follow, she generally kept abolitionism out of her writings for children.[48]

R—ROLAND REMPLIT UN POT POUR Y PLANTER SON ROSIER.

REFERENCES

1. *See* Baer, Helen G. *The Heart Is Like Heaven: The Life of Lydia Maria Child.* Philadelphia, University of Pennsylvania Press, 1964; and Meltzer, Milton. *Tongue of Flame: The Life of Lydia Maria Child.* New York, Crowell, 1965. Both of these published biographies are anecdotal and sentimental. Better than either are: Lamberton, Berenice G. "A Critical Biography of Lydia Maria Child." Ph.D. diss., University of Maryland, 1953; and Taylor, Lloyd C. "To Make Men Free: A Biography of Lydia Maria Child." Ph.D. diss., Lehigh University, 1956. For good brief treatments, *see* Thorp, Margaret Farrand. *Female Persuasion: Six Strong-Minded Women.* New Haven, Conn., Yale University Press, 1949, pp. 215-53;

Conrad, Susan Phinney. *Perish the Thought: Intellectual Women in Romantic America, 1830-1860.* New York, Oxford University Press, 1976, pp. 104-16; Jeffrey, Kirk. "Marriage, Career, and Feminine Ideology in Nineteenth-Century America: Reconstructing the Marital Experience of Lydia Maria Child, 1828-1874," *Feminist Studies* 2:113-30, 1975; and Filler, Louis. "Child, Lydia Maria (Francis)," *Notable American Women: A Biographical Dictionary.* Cambridge, Mass., Belknap Press of Harvard University Press, 1971, vol. 1, pp. 330-33.

2. For information about how other children's writers handled slavery, *see* Crandall, John C. "Patriotism and Humanitarian Reform in Children's Literature, 1825-1860," *American Quarterly* 21:3-22, Spring 1969; and MacLeod, Anne Scott. *A Moral Tale: Children's Fiction and American Culture, 1820-1860.* Hamden, Conn., Archon Books, 1975, pp. 111-16.

3. Baer, op. cit., p. 25.

4. Meltzer, op. cit., pp. 4-6.

5. Lamberton, op. cit., pp. 9-10, 20. *See also* "The Indian Boy," *Juvenile Miscellany* 2:30-31, May 1827; and "Pol Sosef: The Indian Artist," *Juvenile Miscellany*, n.s., 5:280, Jan. 1831.

6. Lamberton, op. cit., p. 26.

7. Dall, Caroline H. "Lydia Maria Child and Mary Russell Mitford," *Unitarian Review and Religious Magazine* 19:525-26, June 1883.

8. In a random survey, I counted nineteen stories from the *Miscellany* in a single volume of the *Youth's Companion*, vol. II, May 30, 1828-May 21, 1829, and five in *Merry's Museum*, vol. 17, Jan.-July 1849, one of which was unacknowledged. Revealingly, however, none of the borrowed stories deals with slavery.

9. "Address to the Young," *Juvenile Miscellany* 1:iii-iv, Sept. 1826.

10. MacLeod, op. cit.

11. Ibid., p. 148.

12. "Value of Time," *Juvenile Miscellany* 1:103-05, Jan. 1827. *See also* "Time and Money," *Juvenile Miscellany*, n.s., 2:218-26, July 1829.

13. "The French Orphan, or...The New Year's Reward," *Juvenile Miscellany* 1:1-18, Jan. 1827.

14. "The Cottage Girl," *Juvenile Miscellany*, n.s., 1:5, 7-8, Sept. 1828. *See also* Gaskell, Elizabeth. *Mary Barton.* London, Chapman and Hall, 1848; reprinted in 1970 by Penguin Books, edited and with a fine introduction by Stephen Gill.

15. "Cottage Girl," op. cit., p. 16.

16. Child, Lydia Maria. *The First Settlers of New-England: or, Conquest of the Pequods, Narrangansets and Pokanokets: As Related by a Mother to Her Children, and Designed for the Instruction of Youth.* Boston, Munroe and Francis, and Charles S. Francis, n.d., pp. iii-iv. The Library of Congress has penciled in the date 1828?, but in his bibliography, Whittier lists the date 1829. *See* Whittier, John Greenleaf, ed. *Letters of Lydia Maria Child.* Boston, Houghton, Mifflin, 1883; reprinted, New York, Negro Universities Press, 1969, p. 272.

17. Child, *First Settlers*, op. cit., pp. 281-82.

18. "Adventure in the Woods," *Juvenile Miscellany* 1:1-13, Sept. 1826.

19. "American History," *Juvenile Miscellany*, n.s., 2:202-05, May 1829; and 2:319-23, July 1829.

20. Ibid., pp. 320-21.

21. "The Indian Boy," op. cit., pp. 28-31; and "Pol Sosef," op. cit., pp. 278-79.

22. My count is based on a thorough canvass of all 16 volumes of the *Miscellany*. I am including a few selections by other contributors, on the assump-

tion that Child's principles would have led her to reject any contributions she found morally objectionable. I am also excluding one selection, not by Child, but probably consonant with her views at the time (1827), because it minimizes the evils of slavery.

23. Crandall, op. cit., pp. 12-18; and MacLeod, op. cit., pp. 111-16.

24. MacLeod, op. cit., pp. 112, 114-15.

25. Child, Lydia Maria. *An Appeal in Favor of [That Class of] Americans Called Africans.* 1833; reprinted, New York, Arno Press, 1968, preface.

26. Ibid., p. 195.

27. "William Peterson, the Brave and Good Boy," *Juvenile Miscellany*, 3d ser., 6:66-67, March 1834.

28. "New Books," *Juvenile Miscellany*, 3d ser., 2:320-21, July 1832.

29. "Dogs," *Juvenile Miscellany* 4:36-38, March 1828.

30. "Some Talk about Brazil," *Juvenile Miscellany*, 3d ser., 3:31-50, Sept. 1832. *See especially* p. 47; and "Some Talk about Cuba," *Juvenile Miscellany*, 3d ser., 2:198-215, March 1832. *See especially* pp. 214-15.

31. "Some Talk about Brazil," op. cit., p. 47.

32. Compare "Some Talk about Brazil," op. cit., pp. 47-50, with the *Appeal*, op. cit., pp. 186-87; also, compare "Kindness of the Africans," *Juvenile Miscellany*, 3d ser., 5:111-18, Nov. 1833, with the *Appeal*, op. cit., pp. 177-80.

33. "The St. Domingo Orphans," *Juvenile Miscellany*, n.s., 5:81-94, Sept. 1830. Child dates the library privileges extended to her by the Boston Athenaeum from the same period as her meeting with Garrison of approximately 1830; *see* Whittier, ed., op. cit., p. 195. The description of St. Domingo bloodhounds in "Dogs," op. cit., however, suggests that she may have begun reading about slavery even before receiving her library privileges.

34. "St. Domingo Orphans," op. cit., p. 91.

35. Ibid., pp. 91-92.

36. Ibid., p. 94.

37. MacLeod, op. cit., p. 115; and Crandall, op. cit., p. 15.

38. *See* "The Unfortunate Moor," *African Repository* 3:364-67, Feb. 1828; "Abduhl Rahahman, the Unfortunate Moorish Prince," *African Repository* 4:77-81, May 1828; "Abduhl Rahahman, the Unfortunate Moor," *African Repository* 4:243-50, Oct. 1828; "Unfortunate Moorish Prince," *Youth's Companion* 2:25-26, July 11, 1828; and "Slavery," *Youth's Companion* 2:32, July 18, 1828.

39. "The Unfortunate Moor," op. cit., p. 365.

40. "Slavery," op. cit. This conservative position was standard antislavery doctrine for the 1820s, and Child herself expressed views very similar to this in *Evenings in New England. Intended for Juvenile Amusement and Instruction. By an American Lady* (Boston, Cummings, Hilliard, 1824, pp. 138-39). But by 1831, the date of "Jumbo and Zairee," she had moved far beyond this, and by 1833, she was fully committed to immediate abolition, the Garrisonian solution. Meanwhile, Nathaniel Willis, editor of the *Youth's Companion*, continued to regard immediate abolition as dangerous and impracticable.

41. "Jumbo and Zairee," *Juvenile Miscellany*, n.s., 5:291, Jan. 1831.

42. Ibid., pp. 285, 290-91.

43. Ibid., pp. 296-99.

44. *See* Child, Lydia Maria. *Anti-Slavery Catechism.* Newburyport, Mass., Charles Whipple, 1836. *See especially* p. 35, for a concise statement of abolitionist doctrine, at least as she defined it. As an abolitionist, Child still sought the

voluntary conversion of slaveholders like Mr. Harris, but on a larger scale: "The abolitionists...merely wish to *induce the Southerners to legislate for themselves*; and they hope to do this by the universal dissemination of facts and arguments, calculated to promote a *correct public sentiment* on the subject of slavery" (italics in original).

45. "Mary French and Susan Easton," *Juvenile Miscellany*, 3d ser., 6:186-202, May 1834.

46. Ibid., p. 202.

47. *Juvenile Miscellany*, 3d. ser., vol. 6, no. 3, July 1834, note at the end of the volume.

48. In the 1840s, Child reissued some of her *Miscellany* stories, along with some new ones, in three volumes entitled *Flowers for Children* (New York, C.S. Francis; Boston, J.H. Francis, 1844, 1845, 1847). She included only one of her antislavery stories (and one of the least interesting), "The Little White Lamb and the Little Black Lamb" (*Juvenile Miscellany*, 3d ser., 4:53-56, March 1833), toning down its moral. And among the new stories only one—"Lariboo. Sketches of Life in the Desert"—had an African setting, but no real antislavery commentary. See *Flowers for Children*, vol. 2, pp. 132-34, and vol. 3, pp. 153-84. Three of Child's four subsequent volumes of children's stories contained no antislavery pieces. The last, however, *The Children of Mount Ida and Other Stories* (New York, Charles S. Francis, 1871), contained two very interesting ones: "The Quadroons" (pp. 61-76) and "The Black Saxons" (pp. 190-204).

S—SUSETTE A UN MORCEAU DE SUCRE POUR SON SERIN.

T—THÉRÈSE EST TRISTE PARCEQUE SON TABLIER EST SALE.

Idealization of the Child and Childhood in Frances Hodgson Burnett's *Little Lord Fauntleroy* and Mark Twain's *Tom Sawyer*

PHYLLIS BIXLER

The following discussion of idealization of the child in Frances Hodgson Burnett's *Little Lord Fauntleroy* (1886) and idealization of childhood in Mark Twain's *Tom Sawyer* (1876) is part of a larger study of the pastoral tradition in children's classics. The impetus for this study came primarily from three sources: William Empson's essay on *Alice in Wonderland* in *Some Versions of Pastoral*;[1] the fact that two of the most important works for an understanding of modern literary portrayals of the child, Rousseau's *Émile* (1762) and Wordsworth's *Prelude* (1805, 1850), associated childhood with a natural setting; and the significant number of children's classics which similarly portrayed the

85

child or had pastoral themes—works such as *Tom Sawyer* and *Huckleberry Finn* (1885); *Heidi* (1880, English translation 1884); *Peter Pan* (1904); *The Secret Garden* (1911); the Laura Ingalls Wilder series (1932-43); *The Wind in the Willows* (1908); Milne's Winnie-the-Pooh books (1926, 1928); *The Hobbit* (1938); and *Charlotte's Web* (1952).

Empson's definitions of pastoral and the child as a pastoral figure proved too broad for my purposes; I found it more helpful to distinguish two kinds of traditional pastoral ideals: the bucolic ideal, based on Theocritus's *Idylls* and Virgil's *Eclogues*, both of which depicted shepherd life; and the georgic ideal, based on Virgil's *Georgics*, which described the farmer's life. I noted ways in which these traditional ideals could be considered childlike and thus could be attributed to the child and childhood both by Rousseau and Wordsworth and in children's literature.[2]

Signatures of the traditional bucolic ideal, based on the shepherd's life, include a receiving of nature's sustenance with a minimum of work, an easy companionship with friends with a minimum of social responsibility, and an immersion in the present with little sense of passing time. In summary, the bucolic ideal represents a holiday from many of life's often unpleasant realities. In Renato Poggioli's words, "the psychological root" of this ideal is "a double longing after innocence and happiness to be recovered not through conversion or regeneration but merely through retreat."[3] The traditional georgic ideal, based on the farmer's life, however, stresses a cooperative relationship between man and nature, between man and man. Within the social institutions of family and community, man works to help nature yield its bounty. Man's work and social life are determined by the seasonal cycle, and this yearly experience of nature's death and rebirth is often paralleled by an individual or social experience of renewal or rebirth.

The georgic ideal found expression in nineteenth-century children's religious, especially evangelical, literature, which portrayed the child who is converted and then through preaching or example helps convert others, adults as well as children.[4] As Gillian Avery has noted, this religious concept underwent a romantic secularization and stressed other beneficent effects children could have on adults.[5] Through his innocence and vulnerability, for example, the child could give new meaning to the life of a misanthropic adult. Such a child is Eppie in George Eliot's *Silas Marner* (1861), which has as its epigraph a quotation from Wordsworth's "Michael": "A child, more than all other gifts/That earth can offer to declining man,/Brings hope with it, and forward-looking thoughts." Within children's literature, examples include the main characters of George MacDonald's *At the Back of the North Wind* (1871) and Johanna Spyri's *Heidi,* as well as of Burnett's *Little Lord Fauntleroy, A Little Princess* (1905), and *The Secret Garden.* Congruent with the social emphasis of the georgic ideal, the child in these works often acts as the agent of rebirth in others by becoming the focal character of a family or other small community. The home, sometimes associated with a rural or other green place, thus becomes the primary pastoral oasis within which redemption occurs. Since it portrays an exemplary rather than a typical child, one whose virtues are worthy and capable of adult emulation even though they may be especially associated with children, this georgic idealization of the child does not represent an idealization of childhood itself.

The bucolic portrait, on the other hand, does often purport to be that of the typical or quintessential child, and thus idealizes childhood itself. Bucolic ideals, such as freedom from work and social responsibility and an immersion in the present moment, are qualities of life suggested to be the exclusive property of childhood. Children are portrayed as happiest and most fully themselves when they are playing, free from adult intrusion. The ideal community is not the family, but a group of children who consider adults an alien order of being, with whom they play a "we versus they" game. They ridicule the model child who embodies the virtues adults value, and they flout adult restrictions, especially those arising from the claims of family, religion, and school.

Compared to georgic idealizations of the child, bucolic idealizations of childhood imply a greater difference between childhood and adulthood and thus place a greater emphasis on what it means to grow up. Often, they focus on some way of marking the difference between childhood and adulthood—such as going to school, ceasing to believe in fairies, sexual initiation—some gate which, once passed, cuts the adult off from the joys of childhood except through nostalgic memories. The sadness of this vision is vividly depicted by the adult narrator of one of the fullest expressions of this bucolic idealization of childhood, Kenneth Grahame's *The Golden Age* (1895). As this "Olympian"—so Grahame labels the adult—gazes back over his lost childhood, he muses: "Somehow the sun does not seem to shine so brightly as it used; the trackless meadows of old time have shrunk and dwindled away to a few poor acres. A saddening doubt, a dull suspicion, creeps over me. *Et in Arcadia ego*—I certainly did once inhabit Arcady. Can it be that I also have become an Olympian?"[6] This bucolic "longing for innocence and happiness" through a "retreat" into an idealized childhood finds expression in children's works such as Catherine Sinclair's *Holiday House* (1839) and Flora Shaw's

Castle Blair (1878) as well as in better-known classics such as *Alice in Wonderland* (1865), *Peter Pan*, Milne's Winnie-the-Pooh books, *Tom Sawyer*, and *Huckleberry Finn*.

As my primary example of the georgic idealization of the child in nineteenth-century children's literature, I will discuss only *Little Lord Fauntleroy*, the book which first won Frances Hodgson Burnett fame as a best-selling author. However, two other children's works for which she is well known, *A Little Princess* and *The Secret Garden*, also fit into this georgic category.[7] Moreover, in her childhood memoir, *The One I Knew Best of All: A Memory of the Mind of a Child* (1893), Burnett shows the influence of two literary traditions I have identified as crucial in nineteenth-century idealized portraits of the child: religious stories about exemplary children and the romantic association of childhood with a natural setting, as in Rousseau's *Émile* and Wordsworth's *Prelude*. In her memoir, Burnett was highly critical of the religious exempla she had read as a child. She described them as "horrible little books" about "dreadful children who died early of complicated diseases, whose lingering developments they enlivened by giving unlimited moral advice and instruction to their parents and immediate relatives."[8]

> In "Little Saint Elizabeth" (1890), the story of a child whose good instincts are warped by her aunt's religiosity and by the many legends of saints she has read, Burnett similarly scorned the excesses of the religious exempla as well as the attempts to imitate them too literally and self-consciously. Despite such harsh criticism, however, Burnett returned to this genre repeatedly in her memoir; like Little Saint Elizabeth, she had been much affected by the religious stories she had read. She knew as a child that she could not match the fictional children in their high standards of conduct or in their ability to effect instant conversion in others.[9]

Nevertheless, "there was nothing she would have been so thankful for as to find that she might attain being an Example."[10]

Burnett's memoir also shows the influence of the romantic association of childhood with a pastoral setting. She describes an "enchanted garden" she played in as a child, a garden she ironically labels the "Back Garden of Eden" because there a childish peccadillo—she accepted a candy "on trust," without paying for it—was magnified by her overdeveloped conscience into "the first Crime of her infancy." Later, in an episode which foreshadows her famous fictional "secret" garden, she depicts her delight in a long-locked and abandoned garden she discovered near her home in Manchester, England. And finally, she devotes a long chapter to the formative effect the forests and mountains of Tennessee had on her as an adolescent.[11] Like Wordsworth, she would have us believe that her imagination was early formed by nature.

The extended use of nature in a portrayal of the child would wait until Burnett's masterpiece, *The Secret Garden*. All three of her best-known children's works, however, show the influence of the religious exemplum and thus bear marks of what I call the georgic idealization of the child; that is, they portray children who are the agents of rebirth in others, in part because they become the focal characters of a family or other small community. In *A Little Princess*, Sara befriends other orphans and beggars before she is adopted by the wealthy recluse next door whose health and happiness she strengthens. In *The Secret Garden*, Mary's reviving touch with nature becomes a model for the invalid Colin; together, the two children bring psychological healing to Colin's father. Cedric Errol, in *Little Lord Fauntleroy*, is an earlier version of this georgic portrait. At the beginning of the tale, this seven-year-old child is a victim. His paternal grandfather is a wealthy English lord, but Cedric and his mother live in considerable poverty in New York City, since Cedric's father, now dead, had been disinherited for marrying a woman who was both American and an orphan. All of the English lord's heirs die, however, and so he sends for little Cedric, though he still refuses to see Cedric's mother. Cedric's grandfather proves to be a gouty, irascible recluse—the perfect object for for a georgic child's saving powers. The lord's first interest in Cedric is purely selfish—he wants an heir. But Cedric's unconscious innocence wins the lord to a genuine affection for the boy, an affection which has a more general redemptive effect on his misanthropic nature. For example, Cedric gets his grandfather to improve the conditions of his tenants, and Cedric also manages a rapprochement between his grandfather and his mother. The tale ends with a birthday party for the new Little Lord Fauntleroy, a celebration not only for the newly reformed family, but also for the rural community in and around the lord's estate.

The beneficent effect Little Lord Fauntleroy has on those about him clearly marks his portrait as a georgic idealization of the child. Moreover, he has a winning effect on others because of his exemplary qualities. First, he is innocent. As Burnett said of her own son, who was the model for her literary creation, Fauntleroy "was born without sense of the existence of any barrier between his own innocent heart and any other."[12] He is a friend of the whole world because he considers everyone in the world his friend. He brings out the good in his grandfather by simply assuming his grandfather is good. Moreover, Cedric's innocence is incorruptible; he proves incapable of being "bought" by his grandfather. Told that he can have anything he wants, Cedric asks mainly for gifts for others. In addition, Little Lord Fauntleroy is pretty; if the reader of Burnett's text forgot the importance of Cedric's ringlets and velvet suits, Reginald Birch's illustrations for the first editions were reminders.

As is well known, the same exemplary innocence and beauty which brought Cedric friendship and fame within Burnett's fiction brought him notoriety as a "sissy" among a generation of boys whose parents apparently believed they could make their children innocent by giving them Fauntleroy's hairstyle and dress. "A justifiable sympathy for these real-life victims probably played a significant role in the unjustifiably negative criticism and reputation Burnett's book has sometimes received."[13] The book itself, as Gillian Avery has noted, remains "curiously compelling"[14] despite the fact that styles in children and children's clothes have changed. To understand why, one must cease trying to read it as realistic fiction and rather regard it as a frankly idealized portrait of a child which is making a symbolic statement. *Little Lord Fauntleroy* compels much as does "another story which has suffered from too-literal interpretations, the Clerk's Tale in Chaucer's *Canterbury Tales*. The Patient Griselda, like Little Lord Fauntleroy, has been deplored by readers as a monster of virtue despite the Clerk's declaration that he meant his tale to be taken not as an example of wifely behavior but as an inspiration to steadfastness in the tests which God sends us."[15] Similarly, *Little Lord Fauntleroy* depicts the age-old theme of the testing of virtue. Cedric Errol must pass one test after another to show that he is "innocent" and "every inch a lord." He must not allow his affections to be bought; he must not be sullen and angry because he is separated from his mother, his "Dearest"; he must face the threat of an imposter heir with grace and equanimity. Like so much of early children's literature, Burnett's story is an exemplum. But it compels because it returns to an earlier use of that form— not to demonstrate or inculcate specific modes of behavior but to make a symbolic statement about the power of virtue.[16]

While Burnett used the exemplary child in religious literature as a basis for her georgic idealization of the child in *Little Lord Fauntleroy*, Mark Twain turned the religious model-child upside down as part of his bucolic idealization of childhood in *Tom Sawyer*. Ten years before finishing *Tom Sawyer*, Twain spoofed the religious exemplum in his "Story of a Bad Little Boy" and "The Story of a Good Little Boy." In the former sketch, the "bad little boy" commits most of the Sunday-school-book sins with impunity; in the latter, the "good little boy" gets into trouble for doing the prescribed good deeds. Similarly, in *Tom Sawyer*, Twain satirizes the good child in Tom's tattletale brother Sid as well as in the "model boy," Willie Mufferson, who always accompanies his mother to church and whom all the boys hate because he is so good.[17] In Tom Sawyer himself, Twain elevates the "bad boy"—the boy who smokes, steals, lies, fights, disrupts school and church, plays hookey—into a new kind of ideal boy. In doing so, Twain joined a series of post-Civil War books headed by Thomas Bailey Aldrich's *The Story of a Bad Boy* (1869), novels and memoirs which celebrated the "bad boy" as the quintessential American boy.[18]

Twain's quintessential American boy is not only "bad" but also "natural." He has his source not only in religious exempla but also in the romantic pastoral tradition of portraying childhood as a time of especial affinity with nature. When they can, Tom and his friends play on Cardiff Hill, that "delectable land," "green with vegetation," which lies "dreamy, reposeful, and inviting" beyond and above the village. In addition, the boys enjoy Jackson's Island. After a day of games and swimming and a night of peaceful sleep, Tom wakes to watch "the cool gray dawn," "the delicious sense of repose and peace in the deep pervading calm and silence of the woods" where "not a sound obtruded upon great Nature's meditation."[19]

It is especially within such natural settings that Twain's boys experience the bucolic joys which are the special province of childhood, primarily freedom from work and social responsibilities. In traditional bucolic poems, this ideal of a life with minimal tension and action—the ideal obviously excluded heroic action—was called *otium*. Originally a military term, *otium* was the antonym of *negotium*, which meant "duty." Thus, the bucolic shepherd was one who was "at liberty" or on leave from duty.[20] Accordingly, the bucolic ideal can be described as a holiday defined primarily by negatives; that is, it is defined not so much by what one does as by what one does *not* do—one's usual duties. It emphasizes freedom *from* more than freedom *to*.

This bucolic ideal of *otium* aptly describes the boys' life on Jackson's Island. Since they have "hooked" bacon and ham from Aunt Polly's larder, and since the river yields a plentiful supply of fish, they have little work to do. Moreover, they are "playing hookey" from the social institutions of school and family as well as from adults whose restrictions support these institutions. Like bucolic shepherds, Twain's boys are free to do pretty much as they like. They can swim, play marbles, pretend to be circus clowns and pirates—or experience the *otium* of doing nothing at all. The option to do nothing, as well as the definition of their holiday through negatives, is demonstrated by Tom's joyful description of their life to his fellow "pirates" on the island: "It's just the life for me....You *don't have to* get up, mornings, and you *don't have to* go to school, and wash, and all that blame foolishness [emphasis added]. You see a pirate don't have to do *anything*...when he's ashore."[21]

Twain's boys soon find out, however, that their bucolic idyll on Jackson's Island cannot last forever, even if they wanted it to. As critics of traditional pastoral poetry have recognized, the bucolic ideal is "a paradise of our hopes and wishes"[22] that can be experienced, if at all, only in intermittent moments and under very special conditions. Because of these special conditions—freedom from work and social responsibility, and, often, immunity from time and change—a literary portrayal of the bucolic ideal must posit a very special "landscape." Thomas G. Rosenmeyer borrowed from Spenser the term *green cabinet* to describe this literary pastoral landscape.[23] The word *cabinet* suggests both the relative smallness of the pleasance and the fact that it is an enclosed place— much is excluded. The cabinet has "walls" that act as artificial boundaries to keep out the harsher realities of life which would destroy the enjoyment of the bucolic ideal. These walls must be respected if the idyll is to continue. The words *idyll* and *pastoral poem* have sometimes been used to describe *Tom Sawyer;* Twain himself once called it a "hymn."[24] The concept of a literary pastoral as a "green cabinet" can be used to examine the extent to which Twain's book as a whole—not just the Jackson Island episodes—can be called a bucolic idyll of childhood, a book in which "the dreams of all childhood everywhere are fulfilled," to quote Bernard DeVoto, despite the "dread and horror" at the root of some of Tom's adventures.[25]

The "walls" of Twain's "green cabinet," the boundaries which protect his bucolic idyll of childhood, can be identified if we see the resemblances of the idyll to a game. There are precedents within the pastoral tradition for this method of presenting the bucolic ideal. Speaking of classic bucolic poetry, Rosenmeyer says that the shepherds' songs and the bucolic poems as a whole are "often curiously like the simple phrases of children's songs and games"; it is as if "the pastoral singer had...decided that art was indeed a children's game, and that only a children's game was true art."[26] In games, boundaries are set by certain established rules. These rules give order to the game. In addition, they keep the game a game: if the contestants exceed the boundaries set by these rules, their battle is no longer an imaginary one; it is real. When this happens in a bucolic idealization of childhood, the idyll will be broken.

The bucolic holidays Twain's boys enjoy when they are by themselves, as well as their usual relationships with adults, can be seen as games. Most of the rules for these games are determined by the restrictions which adults normally impose upon the boys. As already noted, the boys define their bucolic holiday by a negation of these adult restrictions, and they also ultimately find that their enjoyment is dependent on the restrictions. Joe Harper says: "Swimming's no good. I don't seem to care for it, somehow, when there ain't anybody to say I shan't go in." In another context, Tom discovers the importance of prohibitions in his enjoyment of such pleasures as smoking, chewing and swearing. After he leaves the order of the Cadets of Temperance and is no longer under a promise not to indulge in these vices, he finds he no longer wants to. The famous scene in which Tom gets his friends to whitewash the fence by suggesting that he should not let them do it illustrates beautifully the way in which rules define not only work but also play. In the words of the "great and wise philosopher" who was recording Tom's adventures: "Work consists of whatever a body is *obliged* to do, and....Play consists of whatever a body is not obliged to do."[27]

Since the bucolic play which children enjoy when they are by themselves is so dependent on adult restrictions, it hardly represents a genuine rebellion against adult and social authority. No doubt that is why their "playing hookey" is so readily tolerated by adults and society. Moreover, the battles which the child fights with adults are not genuine hostilities but rather a game. All sorts of naughty behavior, all sorts of playing around with adult restrictions, can be tolerated so long as the child does not *intend* to do wrong or to hurt. If one *meant* to hurt, of course, the game battle would become real; the rule of not intending to hurt thus acts as the outer boundary within which the game can safely be played. This rule clearly obtains in the skirmishes between Tom and Aunt Polly. After staying on Jackson's Island and making Aunt Polly think he is dead, and after making a fool of her by convincing her that he dreamed he visited her to comfort her, Tom wins Aunt Polly's affectionate forgiveness by saying that he "didn't think" and "didn't mean to be mean." Aunt Polly makes a similar appeal to explain her apparently hostile actions toward Tom. When Tom reproves her for giving him medicine which "roasted his bowels out of him," Aunt Polly realizes that she had not before considered that her actions might have been cruel, and she tells Tom, "I was meaning for the best."[28] The fact that Tom's battle with adults is only a game, that he accepts adult restrictions even as he is overturning them, is reinforced by the final scene in the book. Tom will not allow Huck to join his gang of robbers unless Huck returns to the Widow Douglas and becomes "respectable"; Huck must do all the things Tom himself enjoyed *not* doing on Jackson's Island—getting up in the morning, going to school, and washing. To summarize, the "we versus they" game Tom plays with adults never becomes real enough to break Twain's bucolic idyll of childhood.

There is another kind of game in *Tom Sawyer*, however, which does become almost too real and thus threatens to break Twain's bucolic idealization of childhood. Tom and his friends play imaginary games in which they act out the adventures of knights, pirates, and robbers Tom has read about in books. Often, these imaginary adventures serve to reinforce the dominant bucolic ideal by mocking its opposite, the heroic ideal. The grandeur of the children's imaginary heroism is undercut by reminders that these are, after all, just children. On Jackson's Island, for example, the "Black Avenger" and the "Terror of the Seas" throw up after smoking, and get homesick; these "pirates" secretly say their prayers and worry about having stolen bacon and ham from home. These imaginary adventures do threaten Twain's idyll in that they lead Tom and Huck, indirectly at least, into the "dread and horror" of their encounter with the real murderer and robber, Injun Joe. In a number of respects, the boys' involvement in Injun Joe's affairs can be seen as an example of children's play becoming real. First, the boys witness Injun Joe's heinous deeds while they are playing. Second, the Injun Joe plot itself is an outgrowth of the games the boys play. They go to the graveyard to cure their warts by throwing a dead cat at the devil, and a real devil appears in the form of Injun Joe. Later, while they are searching an abandoned house for robbers' treasure, they discover real robbers and real treasure.

Twain manages to keep the Injun Joe plot largely within his bucolic "green cabinet," however, by not making it distinct enough from the imaginary outlaw games which children play. Injun Joe is too much like the kind of melodramatic villain which Tom would be likely to conjure up in his own superstitious and imaginary games. And the boys' role in the affair turns on too many coincidences for us to take the dangers of this adventure very seriously. Similarly, the other flirtations with tragedy in the book, such as the funeral for the "dead" boys and the escape from the cave, are too much like the acting out of children's fantasies to pose a serious threat to Twain's idyll. To paraphrase Rosenmeyer on the bucolic poem as whole and the shepherd's songs within the poem, Twain's book as a whole, as well as the children's play within that book, are curiously like children's games.[29]

Huckleberry Finn, of course, represents a dramatic example of what happens to the bucolic idyll of childhood when the child's imaginary games do become real. Huck plays hookey from family and school for his own survival; he becomes a real rather than an imaginary outlaw. To remind us of this contrast, Twain opens his novel with a portrayal of Tom playing his imaginary games. Later, Twain has Huck say of his escape from his father's cabin, "I did wish Tom Sawyer was there, I knowed he would take an interest in this kind of business, and throw in the fancy touches."[30] For Huck, the "we versus they" game which Tom played with adults also becomes real. Huck refuses to become "respecta-ble." His adventures represent no temporary overturning of the rules but an open questioning of them. Especially when Huck's refusal to be "respectable" means questioning the law of slavery and abetting a runa-way slave, it is clear that he is questioning not just adult authority but the authority of society itself. As Huck moves on the raft down the Mississippi River, he is on a collision course against society, and Mark Twain has a real hero, not a mock hero, on his hands. His idyll of childhood is turning into a nightmare.

The ending of *Huckleberry Finn*, as is well known, has received almost endless critical commentary.[31] Specifically, critics have felt that Huck's willingness to participate in Tom's fanciful but cruel schemes for "freeing" Jim from jail is inconsistent with Huck's earlier friendship with the runaway slave, even as Huck's cooperation is a betrayal of the vision he gained during his heroic journey. The preceding discussion of *Tom Sawyer* provides perhaps another way of describing the problems of this ending. To avoid Huck's collision with society, Twain puts him where he will not hurt anybody or himself—back in Tom's bucolic childhood world where heroism is only imaginary and battles with adults and society are only a game. Moreover, he suggests that Huck need not grow up but can roam eternally in that idealized antebellum "territory" of childhood. In other words, Twain tries to turn his nightmare back into an idyll by returning to the bucolic idealization of childhood he celebrated in *Tom Sawyer*.

REFERENCES

1. Empson, William. *Some Versions of Pastoral*. Reprinted, New York, New Directions, 1974.

2. Especially helpful in arriving at these definitions of the bucolic and georgic ideals were: Poggioli, Renato. *The Oaten Flute: Essays on Pastoral Poetry and the Pastoral Ideal*. Cambridge, Mass., Harvard University Press, 1975; and Rosenmeyer, Thomas G. *The Green Cabinet: Theocritus and the European Pastoral Lyric*. Berkeley, University of California Press, 1969. For a fuller discussion of these ideals, and especially their role in the portrayal of childhood by Rousseau, Wordsworth, and a variety of children's writers, *see* Koppes, Phyllis Bixler. "The Child in Pastoral Myth: A Study in Rousseau and Wordsworth, Children's Literature and Literary Fantasy." Ph.D. diss., University of Kansas, 1977.

3. Poggioli, op. cit., p. 1.

4. For a description of this evangelical literature, *see* Avery, Gillian, and Bull, Angela. *Nineteenth Century Children: Heroes and Heroines in English Children's Stories, 1780-1900*. London, Hodder and Stoughton, 1965, pp. 81-93.

5. Ibid., pp. 170-74.

6. Grahame, Kenneth. *The Golden Age*. Reprinted, New York, Avon, 1975, p. 9.

7. For a fuller discussion of these works, *see* Koppes, Phyllis Bixler. "Tradition and the Individual Talent of Frances Hodgson Burnett: A Generic Analysis of *Little Lord Fauntleroy, A Little Princess,* and *The Secret Garden*," *Children's Literature: An International Journal* 7:191-207, 1978.

8. Burnett, Frances Hodgson. *The One I Knew Best of All: A Memory of the Mind of a Child.* New York, Scribner's, 1893, p. 111.

9. Koppes, "Tradition and the Individual," op cit., p. 192.

10. Burnett, op. cit., pp. 188-89.

11. Ibid., pp. 31, 245-60, 251-85. *See also* Koppes, "Tradition and the Individual," op. cit., p. 198.

12. Burnett, Frances Hodgson. "How Fauntleroy Occurred and a Very Real Little Boy Became an Ideal One." In _____ *Piccino and Other Child Stories.* New York, Scribner's, 1894, p. 163.

13. Koppes, "Tradition and the Individual," op. cit., p. 198. In 1932, for example, F.J. Harvey Darton lamented that *Little Lord Fauntleroy* "ran through England like a sickly fever. Nine editions were published in as many months, and the odious little prig in the lace collar is not dead yet." (*Children's Books in England: Five Centuries of Social Life.* Cambridge, University Press, 1932, p. 239).

14. Avery and Bull, op. cit., p. 178.

15. Koppes, "Tradition and the Individual," op. cit., p. 197.

16. *See* ibid., pp. 193-94, 197.

17. Twain, Mark. *The Adventures of Tom Sawyer.* Stormfield ed., New York, Harper, 1876, p. 44. (Reprinted, 1929.)

18. Other examples include: Warner, Charles Dudley. *Being a Boy.* Boston, J.R. Osgood, 1878; Howe, Edgar W. *The Story of a Country Town.* Atchison, Kans., Howe & Co., 1883; and Howells, William Dean. *A Boy's Town.* New York, Harper & Bros., 1890. For a discussion of such books and their relationship to *Tom Sawyer, see* Stone, Albert E., Jr. "Tom Sawyer and His Cousins." In _____ *The Innocent Eye: Childhood in Mark Twain's Imagination.* New Haven, Conn., Yale University Press, 1961, pp. 58-90; and Hunter, Jim. "Mark Twain and the Boy-Book in Nineteenth Century America," *College English* 24:430-38, March 1963.

19. Twain, op. cit., pp. 12, 121.

20. Rosenmeyer, op. cit., p. 67.

21. Twain, op. cit., p. 117.

22. Rosenmeyer, op. cit., p. 18.

23. Ibid., p. vii.

24. DeVoto, Bernard. *Mark Twain at Work.* Cambridge, Mass., Harvard University Press, 1942, pp. 21, 49.

25. Ibid., p. 22.

26. Rosenmeyer, op. cit., p. 56.

27. Twain, op. cit., pp. 138, 185-86, 19.

28. Ibid., pp. 166-67, 108.

29. Rosenmeyer, op. cit., p. 56.

30. Bradley, Edward Sculley, et al., eds. *The Adventures of Huckleberry Finn: An Annotated Text, Backgrounds and Sources, Essays in Criticism.* 1885; reprinted, New York, Norton, 1961, p. 31.

31. *See, for example,* Marx, Leo. "Mr. Eliot, Mr. Trilling, and *Huckleberry Finn,*" *The American Scholar* 22:423-40, Autumn 1953; reprinted in Sculley, et al., op. cit., pp. 328-41.

U—URBAIN A LE DRAPEAU DES ÉTATS-
UNIS.

The Children of Sophie May

CAROL DOLL

In 1863 Lee and Shepard published *Little Prudy*, the first book by the then-unknown Sophie May. Eight years later the *American Literary Gazette* recorded sales of her books had reached 300,000 copies.[1] Her work was reviewed by the magazines and newspapers, and most of the opinions were favorable. In 1866 *The North American Review* said: "Genius comes in with 'Little Prudy.' Compared with her, all other book-children are cold creations of literature only; she alone is the real thing."[2] This paper will consider Sophie May and the children she created.

First, biographical information will be given, although efforts to fill in the facts were not totally successful. However, some correspondence was found which revealed she did not want to write children's books. Then, the major portion of this paper will consider the portrayal of children in Sophie May's books in terms of misbehavior, religion, and style. The patterns discussed in this last section gradually emerged after careful reading of several of her books. Examination of the rest of Sophie May's work helped reinforce and elaborate these basic models.

Sophie May was born Rebecca Sophia Clarke, in Norridgewock, Maine, in 1833, one of four Clarke girls. She was educated at the Norridgewock Female Academy, was tutored in Greek and Latin, and taught in Evansville, Indiana, where a married sister lived. Because of increasing deafness, she quit teaching when she was twenty-eight, and returned to Norridgewock. Short stories she wrote for the religious publications *The Congregationalist* and *The Little Pilgrim* were collected and published as *Little Prudy*. When Rebecca Clarke started to publish her work she needed a pseudonym, so she used her middle name, Sophie. As she tried to think of a last name, she thought that Sophie may or may not write, and created the name Sophie May.[3] Her books were successful, and Lee and Shepard continued to publish her work into the twentieth century. She died on August 16, 1906, after a prolonged illness.

The biographical information available seems to come primarily from two sources, both written more than twenty years after her death. One is an article in the January 1929 issue of *The Maine Library Bulletin*, which includes the journal Rebecca Clarke kept as a child. This journal contains notes on lectures she attended on astronomy and phrenology, and comments on her daily life. The other source is a chapter in the book *Just Maine Folks*, published as a high school text on the history of Maine. These and other articles written from them can only give facts about Rebecca Clarke, but sometimes other sources can be located.

Raymond Kilgour, in his research for *Lee and Shepard: Publishers for the People*, had access to the publishers' files of correspondence, which are in the American Antiquarian Society collections. In Rebecca Clarke's letters to her publisher some of her personality is revealed.

Rebecca Clarke was considered beautiful, with wavy black hair and dark blue eyes. In 1884 after much effort, Lee and Shepard finally obtained a photograph of her to use in its advertising. In the accompanying letter Miss Clarke remarked: "If you'd like my opinion of the lady's face, I think, as my friends do, that it is prettier than mine *ever* was, also sillier; but I hope those curls will please the little folks. If I were to be supposed to wear them now, at my mature age, I *should* be ashamed—but never mind—I'm not yet a hundred."[4]

In September 1867, early in her career, she wrote to offer Lee and Shepard another book, if they were interested. If not, Ashmead and Evans wanted to publish a series. She said: "I told them I preferred my old publishers tho' we had made no definite bargain concerning future books....But, I have no wish to go from my old publishers to new ones unless I have reason to think I can do decidely better....But it does not seem to me a change would do me any good. I like you, and I like your enterprising manner of doing business. I think you have had very much to do with Prudy's success in the world."[5]

Ill health forced Miss Clarke to write slowly, so her average output was two small books and a few short stories per year. In 1868 she wrote: " 'Dotty Dimple at School' is nearly done—has played truant too much, I confess. She is now up to the chin in a snow-drift. What she will fall into next I haven't foreseen. I have exhausted most of the pitfalls, you know, such as fire and water and earthquakes."[6]

Perhaps more clearly than anything else, this correspondence emphasizes Rebecca Clarke's reluctance to produce children's books. She wanted to write for older girls and adults. In 1867 she wrote: "As I did not send you a book last year I thought I would be more enterprising this time and prepare for Christmas. So I summoned courage to undertake a juvenile. You know I have a distaste for Prudy, but looking over one of your old letters, I was struck with your decided preference for her rather than something older, so I concluded to punish myself, and Dotty and Prudy it shall be to the end of the chapter."[7] And two years later, in response to a request for another children's series, she remarked: "But really I don't know what to undertake next. I have not an idea in my head beyond a delicious sense of relief that I have got that everlasting Parlin family tucked away."[8] In 1870 she was still reluctant, but said, "Small children as a rule like repetition, otherwise I should not harbor the idea of more Parlins for a moment."[9]

Lee and Shepard kept prodding and cajoling Rebecca Clarke to write books for children, and published the results as series of six titles each. The Little Prudy Stories, the Dotty Dimple Series, and the Little Prudy's Flyaway Series develop around the adventures of Sister Susy, Little Prudy, and Alice "Dotty Dimple" Parlin and their cousins, Grace, Horace, and Katie "Flyaway" Clifford. The Flaxie Frizzle Stories, named for the blond, curly-haired heroine, center on Mary "Flaxie Frizzle" Gray, and Julia, Preston, Philip and Ethel Gray are also included. The Little Prudy's Children Series was the last one the author wrote, and introduces Kyzie, Jimmy, Lucy, and Eddo Dunlee, Prudy Parlin's children. Besides these main characters each book contains mothers, fathers, grandparents, aunts, uncles, cousins and numerous close friends on a recurring basis. For older girls, Miss Clarke wrote the Quinnebasset Series, which is about young ladies and their families and beaus in a fictional town in Maine. And there were some titles written for adults.

This paper will focus on the portrayal of the children in those titles in the five series designed for "little folks," the Little Prudy Stories, the Dotty Dimple Series, the Little Prudy's Flyaway Series, the Flaxie Frizzle

Stories, and the Little Prudy's Children Series. Specifically, three areas will be discussed: first, the way in which parents and others in authority deal with a child's misbehavior or disobedience; second, an exploration of religion, and in particular church and Sunday school attendance; and finally, an examination of the author's style and method of presenting her characters. There are more possible areas of exploration and research which could be followed, but this project is limited to these three.

In her books, Rebecca Clarke's children go through three distinct stages. Although the boundaries are not always well defined with respect to specific ages, it is not difficult for the reader to determine which child belongs to which stage. Babies are sent down from heaven, and don't usually make major contributions to the story until they begin to walk. The infant stage lasts until they are four or five. During this time, they speak baby talk, get into all kinds of mischief, and tend to be indulged by everyone around them. From the time the children are five or six until they are nine or ten, they are in the junior stage. At this time, they no longer speak baby talk, but tend to make errors in grammar and pronunciation. They begin to develop an active conscience, although they don't always listen to it. Adults expect them to take responsibility for and admit to any misbehavior. By the time children are ten or eleven they are in the adolescent stage. Children speak correctly and have a fully developed conscience. Deliberate misbehavior is rare, but the children still make mistakes and need some guidance. In this stage, they begin to take some responsibility for guiding younger children. The infant stage, junior stage, and adolescent stage are identifiable in the portrayal of children throughout Miss Clarke's work. The three areas of this paper—reaction to misbehavior, religion, and portrayal of characters—will be examined with regard to these three stages.

Authorities in the nineteenth century frequently offered advice to mothers on child rearing. John S.C. Abbott wrote *The Mother at Home,* which "had a very considerable vogue" in the United States and in Europe, according to the *Dictionary of American Biography.* In this book, Abbott stressed to mothers that: "When you do give a command, invariably enforce its obedience. And, God has given every mother the *power.*"[10] The *Dictionary of American Biography* identifies Horace Bushnell as the "pioneer of a new order" of thought for advocating a religious upbringing for children. In *Christian Nurture* he argued, "In every case of discipline for ill-nature, wrong, willfulness, disobedience, be it understood, that the real point is carried never till the child is gentled into love and duty; sorry, in all heartiness, for the past, with a glad mind set to the choice of doing right and pleasing God."[11]

Thus the rational approach was the favored means to guide the child to proper behavior. Punishment itself was not objectionable, as long as the mother could administer it without anger. Self-control, a sensitive conscience, and internalized moral standards were the goal.[12] The hardworking father had little active responsibility, but was supposed to support his wife and provide a good example for his children.

The children in Rebecca Clarke's books are not as strictly stereotyped as the either all-good or all-bad children of earlier writers. That is, her good children are not always angelic; instead they can be, and often are, proud, stubborn, angry, envious and disobedient. This provides frequent opportunity for the child to be disciplined and guided to do what is right, usually following the rational approach advocated by the child-rearing authorities. The mother tries to make the child understand what actions are wrong and why they are wrong. Then the child should feel contrition, ask forgiveness, and finally vow never to do it again. During this process, the conference with the mother or the results of the misbehavior could be considered punishment enough. At other times, additional punishment is deemed necessary. This includes isolation, restriction of movement, denial of a treat or privilege, minor corporal punishment, or something else appropriate to the "crime." Often, the method chosen depends on the age of the child.

When children are in the infant stage, they must begin to control their misbehavior. But adults also realize that perfect behavior can't be expected from these young children. Aunt Madge says: "Nobody thinks any the worse of you to-day for all your baby-mischief....But if you were to do such things now, what *should* we say? Your soul voice would tell you it was wrong, and it would be wrong."[13]

Dotty Dimple is afflicted with a temper which gets out of control. When she was tiny, her sisters would come home to find Dotty on the wood-box in the kitchen, with her hands and feet tied, screaming as loud as possible.[14] When Dotty grew older and could understand more, there were other ways of teaching her to control her temper.

Aunt Madge tells the children about the time when she was little and her mother whipped her for making up a story and threatened another whipping if she ever did it again. Of course, a repeat performance occurred, because Aunt Madge as a child couldn't stop telling those marvelous stories. After the promised switching was administered, her mother decided not to punish Madge anymore until "there was some faint sign in [Madge] that [she] knew the 'difference' between truth and falsehood."[15]

Flaxie Frizzle is a rather strong-minded little girl, who too often gets her own way. When she hits a playmate in *Flaxie Frizzle*, her mother "snips" her hands. But Flaxie is unable to follow the logic of this punishment. If she was naughty for hitting Midge, then mama is naughty for hitting her. Obviously another way to teach and guide Flaxie needs to be found.

As these babies often get into trouble, a frequent, mild punishment is either to lock up or to tie up the disobedient child. In *Flaxie Frizzle* Flaxie goes for an unauthorized ride in her father's carriage. The next day she is tied to the window knob until afternoon. But Flaxie doesn't feel her punishment is too bad, because she has bread and butter to eat while she is there. In *Dotty Dimple's Flyaway* Flyaway is locked in the china closet for half an hour to "think" because she ran away. This doesn't bother her much, because she finds a jar of quince jelly to eat. In *Little Prudy's Dotty Dimple* Dotty is tied to the bedpost for running away to a party her sisters were attending. In *Kyzie Dunlee* Lucy decides it was because of an oversight that she wasn't invited to a party, and decides to go anyway. The next day she is tied to the porch as a punishment. This time her older sister provides the reasoning that helps Lucy understand her misdeed.

Eventually, some of the mothers' efforts to guide and control their children begin to take effect. After Mrs. Gray discovers Flaxie is still too young to have her hands snipped, Flaxie becomes enchanted with husking corn. When Grandfather leaves after feeding the horse, Flaxie carries the ears, one at a time, into her mother, who husks several for her. Finally Mrs. Gray tells Flaxie to take an ear back to the stable and to quit bringing them into the house. But Flaxie insists that her mother has to husk it. Finally Mrs. Gray has to punish her, and locks her in the upstairs bathroom, where Flaxie spends the day insisting her mother husk the corn. Mrs. Gray sits in the next room, greatly distressed and often crying because she has to punish her daughter. Both of them miss dinner, but Flaxie finally goes to sleep and is carried to bed. The next morning she again asks her mother to husk the corn, and then takes the unhusked ear back to the stable: "From this time forth, though often and often a naughty little girl, she never showed any lasting temper, and never gave her mother such serious trouble again."[16]

As the boys and girls grow up, leave behind the infant stage and enter young childhood, different ways of guiding them and correcting misbehavior are used. In *Doctor Papa* Rebecca Clarke remarks, "People told stories to Flaxie when *she* was naughty."[17] This technique seems to be used with the children entering this stage.

In *Dotty Dimple at Home* Dotty, "no longer a mere baby," throws a temper tantrum. Her mother quiets her down, sends her to spend the rest of the morning by herself thinking, and meets her in the nursery after dinner. There Mrs. Parlin tells her the story of Harriet, an orphan who used to "indulge her temper." Harriet consequently beat the baby in her charge so badly that he would never walk again, and she eventually married a Negro fiddler. Dotty retells the story, in a mixed-up fashion, to her sister Prudy, who guides Dotty to resolve not to lose her temper again. Of course this immense problem is not solved so easily, and there is frequent reference to such incidents in the books which follow, but Dotty has made a beginning.

Later, storytelling is less frequent, and a more direct approach is used to guide the children. When she is six, Flaxie Frizzle and her mother discuss Flaxie's behavior while her mother had been away: "These two good friends had a long talk,—the kind mamma and her little daughter who meant to do better,—and when Ninny came to call them to dinner, Flaxie said, joyfully, 'O Ninny, I'm going to begin new, and you mustn't 'member I ever was naughty.' That was the way Mrs. Gray forgave her children; she put their naughtiness far off and never talked of it any more."[18]

At this junior stage, the "little mothers" punish their dolls. In *Wee Lucy's Secret* Lucy decides Dido is "snatching" food at the play luncheon, so the doll is locked in a closet. Later, Phebe "peeks" into the secret chest and Lucy's friend Bab whips the doll. According to Rebecca Clarke, "like many kind-hearted girls, she was extremely severe with her dolls."[19]

When not fighting her temper, Dotty finds plenty of other mischief to keep her busy. While running an errand, Dotty meets Lina Rosenberg, a little Jewish girl. Although she knows her mother would not allow it, Dotty goes to Lina's house. Lina, who thinks she won't have to work while she has a guest, coerces Dotty into staying for dinner. Mr. Parlin finally finds her, but decides to leave her with the Rosenbergs for a while, in spite of Dotty's pleas to return home. After the reunion with her family, Dotty talks with her mother, acknowledges she should have followed her conscience, and vows never to run away again. Mrs. Parlin tells of the distress both parents felt over leaving Dotty with the Rosenbergs. The lesson works, and Dotty doesn't run away again.[20]

As the children grow older, they may be involved in the punishing process. Jimmy and Lucy find a cake in the pantry and sample the frosting in *Jimmy Boy*. Later Jimmy tries to put all of the blame on Lucy. His mother says: "You forgot twice last week to be manly toward Lucy. Is there any way to make you remember?"[21] Together they decide, in spite of some hesitation on Jimmy's part, that he should go without his Fourth of July candy. Eight-year-old Horace finds an opportunity to investigate his mother's watch, and breaks it. The next day his father helps Horace decide that "the little boy who did the mischief should give part of the money" to help repair the watch.[22] This is an especially difficult sacrifice, since Horace's money was for firecrackers.

It is in this junior stage also that the children begin to guide their own behavior. In *Captain Horace* Horace and his sister Grace discuss Horace's behavior, especially such misdeeds as blowing gunpowder, running off into the woods, fishing in his best clothes, and saying bad words. Horace vows to do better, and Grace makes a "merit-book" to keep score. At the end of the month only "bad words" has any marks, and those scores had grown steadily smaller. So Horace was improving on these specific things, even though he did forget and "slammed doors, and lots of things" that Grace didn't put on the list.[23]

In *Prudy Keeping House* Dotty again loses her temper. Little Prudy, Dotty and their cousins, Horace and Flyaway Clifford, are left with the servants when Aunt Madge has to leave. The children decide to play house, and Dotty is angry because she is assigned to be the hired girl, instead of being in charge. She storms upstairs, and rages against Prudy and Horace as she paces her room. Then she sees the card on the wall which says "God resisteth the proud, but giveth grace to the humble." By rather mixed reasoning Dotty applies the verse to herself and decides, "It would be very much better to go back and behave, for I can't stay here without being lonesome."[24] It would seem that over the years Mrs. Parlin's teaching began to take effect. Now Dotty can sometimes apply the technique of rational reasoning to guide herself. When she gets downstairs she finds her role switched from that of hired girl to the more attractive one of lady boarder.

As they grow older and enter the adolescent stage, the children begin to try to help with the little ones. However, they can still make mistakes. When her mother and older sister are both sick, twelve-year-old Flaxie is given "full authority over" Ethel and Phil for the day. Ethel and her cousin, Kittyleen, have a fight over their dolls, and Flaxie decides she must punish Ethel. Flaxie vows, "I'll try to act exactly as mamma always does,—not harsh, but sad and gentle."[25] After a brief discussion, Ethel is left to think over the incident, and consents to write Kittyleen a note forgiving her if Kittyleen will forgive Ethel. The next day Flaxie reports the incident to her mother, who acknowledges that Ethel and Phil were supposed to obey her on the previous day, but denies that Flaxie had the authority to punish them. Because Flaxie didn't shut Ethel in the closet or snip her fingers, Mrs. Gray indicates that Flaxie handled the situation adequately. However, Flaxie is warned against assuming such authority in the future, until she is old enough for the responsibility.

In *Kyzie Dunlee* Mrs. Dunlee is called away to help care for a sick relative. As the oldest, Kyzie is left in charge. Lucy feels that Kyzie doesn't have the authority to make her behave, and so Lucy deliberately misbehaves. Mr. Dunlee then tells Kyzie, "If she gets too troublesome you might, perhaps, shut her up in the closet."[26] After a difficult morning, Lucy makes the baby cry, and Kyzie locks her up in the bathroom. The intended half-hour of isolation becomes an hour and ten minutes, and Lucy decides to take a bath, gets a chill, and develops a bad cold. When Mrs. Dunlee returns, Kyzie pours out the whole story, berating herself relentlessly. Mrs. Dunlee replies: "To be sure you made a mistake in leaving the house after you had locked Lucy into the bathroom. It was a lack of judgment; but that only shows that you are hardly old enough yet to take charge of the family."[27]

Because they are older, the mistakes of children in this adolescent stage are not of the same kind, and different ways of giving guidance are used. In *Little Folks Astray* Aunt Madge tries to tell Horace not to brag about his money in public. He won't listen to her, convinced that he is big enough and smart enough to elude or trap any pickpocket. Predictably, Horace is astounded and very upset when all of the expense money for the trip to New York is missing. Aunt Madge, the amateur pickpocket, returns his money that night, and Horace learns to listen to his aunt when she gives advice.

At this stage also, the children continue to guide themselves. Flaxie vows to give all of her pocket money to a poor family, the Pancakes. She had made a similar proposal earlier, merely to gain the approval of her peers and her Sunday school teacher, and later she regretted this impulsive action and kept the money. This time, however, Flaxie is sincere, and refuses to tell anyone except her mother about her donation, even though her friends probably think she is cold-hearted and stingy. "It was very clear now that Mary had been honestly disgusted with her own conduct, and had chosen this way to punish herself for her false charity and love of display."[28]

In contrast to the good children, Rebecca Clarke's bad children either have no mother to give the necessary guidance, or else the mother, because of ignorance or overwork, does not follow the "recommended" procedure of rational guidance. For example, Mrs. Rosenberg hits her children's hands with a steel thimble. She was "so severe and unreasonable that her little daughter, through fear of her, had learned to deceive."[29] Mrs. Pancake, in regard to her oldest daughter, Pecielena, says, "but she won't mind *me*, sevin (excepting) I licks her."[30] Preston, Flaxie and their friends are not very impressed with this mother. In *Captain Horace* Peter's mother "managed him so badly that he did not care about trying to be good."[31]

At the same time, the heroes and heroines in Rebecca Clarke's books are gently and rationally guided toward good behavior. Mothers, aunts, sisters, grandmothers and, infrequently, fathers and brothers gently admonish, patiently explain and when necessary, coolly, calmly and regretfully administer some punishment. But throughout the books the major emphasis is on the feminine role in guiding the children. For example, Preston is tempted by Tommy Winters to go swimming in the creek in an incident similar to one in *Little Grandfather.* Preston says, "I can't go swimming; mother won't let me." Only after Tommy scornfully says that women are always afraid of the water does Preston say, "Father won't let me either."[32] Fred Allen comes to stay with Dr. Gray's family for a while, and they begin to worry about his behavior. "The boy's manners had been falling to decay all winter for lack of his mother's constant 'line upon line.' "[33] When Fred is called upon to discuss his misbehavior after an April Fool's joke on the minister, the first question is, "Do you think your mother would be pleased to hear of it?"[34] Content analysis of *Little Prudy's Dotty Dimple* reveals that Mrs. Parlin corrected or punished her children six times, Grandmother Read did so twice, the nurse and Aunt Martha once apiece. In addition, Susy and Prudy each correct Dotty once, and three incidents go unpunished.

While recognizing that other patterns of child rearing did exist, Rebecca Clarke's books support the theory of John Abbott and others who recommended gentle, rational and firm methods for rearing children. The "bad" children are raised by other methods. The "good" children are raised in the recommended way, with great emphasis on the feminine role in this better method.

Study of historical children's literature shows that moral tales comprise a large segment of early children's books. There are definitely religious and moral elements in Rebecca Clarke's work. The Little Prudy Stories first appeared in religious publications.[35] While *Dotty Dimple at School* was praised for "moral lessons...beautifully given,"[36] the *Dictionary of American Biography* faults Miss Clarke's work for "obvious moralizing."[37] In 1879 a reviewer asked that she "exclude all reports of the sacred, though it may be amusingly expressed, thoughts which her children may have of God."[38]

References to religion are obviously present in Rebecca Clarke's work. Little Prudy is portrayed as a good little girl who almost never does anything wrong. In *Prudy Keeping House* her hidden strength is revealed. "The secret of Prudy's sweetness was really this: In all trials she was continually saying under her breath, 'Please God, keep me from doing wrong.' She had found that was really the only way—the only safe way."[39] When seven young girls form a club in *Cousin Grace,* they "solemnly pledge...to read two chapters in the Bible daily."[40] In *Little Prudy* Susy remarks, "Mother says if God is willing they'll get well, and if He isn't they'll die. God knows what is best."[41]

At the same time, Rebecca Clarke's bad children have little contact with religion. For example, Peter Grant's cross and ignorant mother "seldom talked with him about God and the Savior; she never read to him from the Bible, nor told him to say his prayers."[42]

In addition to the emphasis on religion, adults and older children try to instill in younger ones a set of morals. Uncle Rufus, while trying to explain God to the four-year-old twins, manages to instill a rudimentary idea of conscience. Later in the book Pollio's understanding increases as his conscience opposes disobedience.[43] Horace is indignant that anyone would even think he could lie. Dotty Dimple's conscience constantly tries to keep her out of mischief, with increasing success. Throughout all Rebecca Clarke's works such incidents are common.

In *The Spiritual Crisis of the Gilded Age* (Northern Illinois University Press, 1971), Paul Carter identifies a number of factors which influenced and upset traditional religion in America from 1865 to approximately 1895. These include the adultery trial of Henry Ward Beecher, the initiation and proliferation of religious fiction, the spread of agnosticism, the splintering off and division of numerous new church groups, a strong anti-Semitic and anti-Catholic prejudice, the rise of biological and social Darwinism, and increased interest in spiritualism. No hint of the social impact of these factors is found in Rebecca Clarke's work for little folks. Yet, she was undoubtedly aware of these issues. This is shown in *Quinnebasset Girls*, where Darwinism is presented as an acceptable theory and the author conveys a disapproval of spiritualism. Perhaps Miss Clarke wished to protect the children in her audience from such unrest. Perhaps she did not wish to confuse them by discussing these issues. Perhaps she felt they were too young. Perhaps there was another reason. This paper will not deal with all of these moral and religious elements. Instead, the following discussion will be limited to specific references to Sunday school and church attendance found in Rebecca Clarke's work.

In the 1800s both church services and Sunday school were part of the child's life, and references to both are included in the journal Rebecca Clarke kept as a child.[44] In her books, church services and Sunday or Sabbath school are portrayed as part of the routine pattern of normal life, and the children's behavior and reaction to incidents in church or Sunday school, or resulting from attendance at either one, are realistically shown. Rebecca Clarke made no effort to sanctify and idealize these religious incidents.

In the infant stage children are not expected to attend either Sunday school or church services because they don't understand yet how to behave. In *Dotty Dimple's Flyaway* Flyaway decides to go to church anyway. The whole family trembles when she appears in Horace's hat with Grandpa's cane and newspaper. Fortunately she falls asleep, with the family's blessing, and doesn't wake up to cause mischief until the service is finished.

Flyaway also has trouble in church in *Prudy Keeping House.* Mrs. Pragoff, a neighbor, decides to take Horace, Prudy, Dotty and Flyaway to a service at Trinity Church to hear the Christmas chimes—and also because she wanted to show off the four children to her friends. Because of prior warnings about Flyaway's inability to sit still and behave, she and Dotty are separated. In spite of this precaution, Flyaway manages to disrupt services by falling off a stool and causing her nose to bleed. All five make a hasty exit, with Flyaway screaming loudly, and Dotty doesn't get to hear the chimes.

Little Prudy and her sister Susy attend Sunday school. Susy's class recites from a question book, and Prudy's class memorizes and discusses Bible verses. Three-year-old Dotty begs to go with them, so one week they take her, too. In Prudy's class Dotty insists on contributing her verse: "What you thpose um had for supper? B'ack-eyed beans, un bread un butter."[45] The class is highly entertained, and Dotty does not attend Sunday school again that year. Furthermore, discussion about the verse "Thy word is a lamp unto my feet, and a light unto my path" activates Dotty's imagination. Her subsequent effort to light a lamp at her feet sets fire to Prudy's dress, and disaster is narrowly averted.

As children leave the infant stage and enter the junior stage, they are expected to go to church and attend Sunday school. And they are expected to behave and pay attention while they are there. While visiting their grandmother, the three Parlin children go to Sunday services with her. Dotty "knew it was wrong to let her thoughts wander when Mr. Preston was speaking to God."[46] But she watches Mr. Gordon, counts the pipes in the organ, and other similar things. Dotty pays attention better in Sunday school, immediately following church services. But she is still too young to understand fully the text, "The Lord loveth a cheerful giver." Later that week she gives her pin money to a beggar, who sneers at the small size of her gift.

In the short story "Kings Cup and Cake," Davy reluctantly goes to church with his family. (This incident is also included in the novel *In Old Quinnebasset.*) Once there he begins to "cut capers," first keeping time to the music, then imitating his sleeping father, and finally aping the deacon. The parson's loud announcement of his name from the pulpit stops his misbehavior, and Davy is ordered to come to the parsonage the next morning. When Davy arrives, the minister guides him through a discussion of the commandments, and elicits a vow for better behavior.

Flaxie Frizzle doesn't always behave in church either. When her little sister, Ethel, goes to church for the first time, nine-year-old Flaxie is very busy watching her, Kittyleen, Sadie, and everything else. She reminds herself, "It's very wicked not to listen."[47] But this self-reproof doesn't improve her behavior. When her father quizzes all of the children on the text of the sermon that night, Flaxie vows to listen very carefully in the future.

Three years later, Flaxie is in the adolescent stage when "she sat in church apparently paying attention to the sermon, but really thinking."[48] She is thinking about how much people must admire her. Later, in Sunday school, she pledges all of her pocket money to help missionaries in China. Her mother's guidance helps Flaxie realize her error in giving only to impress the people around her. (Flaxie eventually punishes herself by keeping secret an act of charity while her friends are planning their own good deeds.)

It isn't necessary for children to attend special services. Phyllis, eleven, and Kyzie, twelve, are left to take care of Lucy and the animals while the Goodwins attend a special service at the church, with visiting ministers and "excellent preaching." The monkey, Jocko, manages to get away from the girls. Just as the choir sings "Spirit of the Lord Come Down," Jocko drops through the skylight and pulls the choir-leader's hair. Mr. Goodwin recaptures Jocko, and takes him home.[49]

In her books Rebecca Clarke dealt with religion, morals, church services, and Sunday school. But the overwhelming, sanctimonious portrayal of religion in the style of the Puritans is gone. Her little folks are characterized as real children, with religion as a part of their lives. Morality and religion are an important part of their training, but they are not so stereotyped as to be totally unbelievable. Rebecca Clarke herself was aware of the possibility of overwhelming her readers with religion and morality. After acknowledging that *Sister Susy* was more moralistic than *Little Prudy*, Rebecca Clarke wrote: "If there is anything stupid it is the *moral influence* which has to be explained on every page. Children skip the moral when it is appended, you know."[50]

Comments on Rebecca Clarke's style can be found in both nineteenth- and twentieth-century publications, especially references to the ungrammatical and babyish speech of her children. One source says, "The characters in her books were largely taken from her nieces and nephews, though she listened to the prattle of any child she chanced to meet and reproduced the quaint and funny sayings, making real children of them."[51] According to a reviewer in *Nation*, Miss Clarke succeeded in creating children with a realistic naturalness.[52] Other disagreed: "We do not think...that children or grown people find the ungrammatical nonsense in print so very charming."[53] Caroline M. Hewins wrote, "Children who are in [third] grade cannot read the ungrammatical baby-talk easily, and if they could it would demoralize their English."[54] The *Dictionary of American Biography* cites the "baby-talk" as one reason for Sophie May's lack of popularity among twentieth-century children.

Careful examination shows three main techniques used by Rebecca Clarke to portray her characters realistically. Small children, especially between the ages of two and four, speak baby talk. Slightly older children, those in the junior stage, make grammatical and vocabulary errors. They also give interesting, although mistaken, explanations to younger children. In the adolescent stage, the children do not make speech or conceptual errors. Instead, they are amused by the mistakes of the younger ones. In addition, Rebecca Clarke wrote in a dialect for Irish, Chinese, Black, Dutch, German, and lower-class characters. And there is evidence that Rebecca Clarke recognized a difference in the regional speech of our country, perhaps due to her stay in Indiana.

Baby talk is restricted to the youngest children. Flaxie Frizzle says, "I's two-uz-ould."[55] The next year Flaxie, using another nickname, dictates a letter to her father:

> MY HEAVEN-MAMMA:—
> I know you's dead and gone to God, but I guess the postman can find you. We's a-goin' to have a Kismus T'ee. I wish you's here to fits it. You s'pose, mamma, when's you comin' down? I kied 'n' kied, 'cause I want to see my mamma. I'se got two kitties in a basket, under um stove; but I want to see my mamma. Tell God 'bout it; then he'll let you come down. Tell him we's a-goin' to have a Kismus T'ee.
> By bye,
PINKY PEARLY[56]

Wee Lucy, jealous of her mother's guitar, decides to get rid of it, and gives it to Santa Claus. Questioned by her mother, Lucy answers: "I tooked it 'way 'way off, mamma; way up to the moon....Sandy Claw lives up in the moon. He tooked it up there where he lives."[57] Baby Eddo, afraid of trains, summons enough courage to shout, "Me s'oot dat Choo Choo with a 'tick o' wood."[58] Four-year-old Dotty, resisting Prudy's efforts to teach reading, rebelliously states, "I don't want to be polite, and speak, nor I don't want to learn my letters, like a goody gell; so there!"[59] Dotty Dimple's request to Flyaway for a kiss is neatly refused. "Can't Dotty Dimpwill! My mamma's kiss I'll keep; it's ahind my mouf."[60]

In those books with the younger children as main or one of several principal characters, such examples of baby talk are abundant. However, it is much less developed in *Little Prudy*, the first of Miss Clarke's works, than in later ones. But in those books featuring older children, the incidence of baby talk is much lower, and tends to be irregular. In *Kyzie Dunlee* Lucy makes several appearances, but there is no baby talk until page 82. In *Jimmy Boy*, also, the amount of Lucy's baby talk is minimal.

When there is a lot of baby talk in a book, Miss Clarke's style is not always consistent. Flaxie says "yiding" for *riding*, and immediately says "right." Wee Lucy says, "Come down yight now," but two pages later pronounces "rain" correctly. After using "pitty" several times, she says "pretty" instead. Baby Eddo switches from "Tum here, little Choo Choo!" to "Come, little Choo Choo." Such lapses are not frequent, but can be found with a little effort. It is difficult to determine whether this is evidence of further effort by Miss Clarke to portray children realistically or an inadvertent mistake.

When characters grow out of the infant stage, baby talk is no longer used. Instead, mispronunciation of longer or less common words prevails, along with some grammatical errors and invented words. For example, Dotty Dimple speaks of "condemned milk" which comes in cans, nervous "exhaustation," and that her memory "preserves" her correctly. Lucy's friend lived in Plaster O' Paris, France, and Colonel Hale buys out their gold mine on "speck-er-lation." Edith "esposes" Lucy to whooping cough, and Jimmy tells her all about Santa Claus, whose "deers have hookers" on their heads. These misuses or mispronunciations of words are frequently isolated, italicized words in the child's normally correct conversation, which makes them easy to identify throughout Miss Clarke's works.

Furthermore, when the children make this type of mistake, they are also likely to make mistakes explaining or understanding things. Prudy solemnly declares she no longer believes the moon to be a chip she threw up in the sky when she was three. Instead, "It's a silver ball as big as a house and there's a man lives there, and I've seen him making up faces."[61] Dotty and her friend Jennie get caught out in a thunderstorm. Jennie explains to Dotty, "in storms like this a conductor is a—a conductor is a—why, I mean if a thing is a conductor, Dotty,—why then the thunder and lightening conducts it all to pieces, and that's the last there is of it."[62] And Susy tells Prudy and Dotty, "This snow has been round on the ground a good while. It's most time it went back to heaven to get clean."[63]

Also in this junior stage, after the grammar and speech patterns improve, the children make numerous errors in writing. Lucy, aged six and a half, has a secret she can't wait to tell Barby, her closest friend. So, in school she uses the slate to pass the message. "When in haste her spelling was always wild....Highrum [Hiram] noes it. Nobody knose it but me and Hierum....New it yistedy. I will tell you....It is a deer little see-crit."[64] In *Doctor Papa*, while Preston, who is ten, takes care of Flaxie, he writes his school composition on apples:

> Apples is the most frout always yoused. Apples is said to grow in almost any country....In some climates it is so warm it is said they have been discovered by the crabapples; they was some men got the seed from the crabapple, and planted it....Some takes the apples, and makes cider of them. Old cider is yoused for vinegar.[65]

In *Twin Cousins* six-year-old Flaxie writes a note to announce her visit:

> Dear Twin Little Cousin: My Mamma is going to let me go to your House and go to school to your Dear teacher, becaus I make too much noise, and Grammy is sick with Something in her back and Ime glad but not unless your Mamma is willing. Wont you please write and say so. My lines are unstraight, and its real too bad Good by
> FLAXIE FRIZZLE[66]

Rebecca Clarke also coined many new cute, catchy words and phrases for her children—not actual words, but with clear meaning: for example, "un-wrong-sided-out," "smile up your face," "blind-eyed," and to be an "own daughter" (instead of adopted).

Although reviewers and biographers fail to mention it, in addition to the baby talk, Rebecca Clarke wrote in a dialect for many of her ethnic and lower-class characters. It is very possible that it never occurred to the reviewers to criticize dialect as we do today. In *Jimmy Boy* and *Kyzie Dunlee* Chinese characters sell "Platoes, sleet corn, cabbage, spinny-gee!"[67] and serve "soup-ee" to a "la-dee."[68] In *Wee Lucy* Molly O'Connor, the maid, talks to Jimmy. "Niver you fret about that, Little Gineral. Santa Claus is rale quick-witted. He'd find *your* house if it was painted up and wheeled off to Africky. Didn't you niver hear about his eyes? It's jist like an owl's eyes they are, made so's to see in the night, right through the top o' the house!"[69] In *Flaxie Frizzle* an Irish peddlar enticing the children with his wares provides a chance for more dialect.

Characters in *Cousin Grace* give opportunity for two more types of dialects. One day Grace loses her ring and accuses Phebe, the black girl who takes care of the baby, of stealing it. Phebe protests, "Why, now, I done declar, Miss Grace, I never took it—never seen it; much as ever I knowed you had a ring....I declar for't, Miss Grace, I hope to die fust!"[70] Another dialect source is Barbara Kinckle, a German Jew who is the Cliffords' hired girl. One night as Grace sits in the kitchen writing a letter, Barby inquires, "Be you writin' to Susy Barlin?" "No, Barby," replies Grace. "Miss Grace, does you write to little Brudy Barlin?"[71]

In *Dotty Dimple Out West* Katinka Dinkelspiel, another German girl, has been hired to replace Barby. Rebecca Clarke remarks, "Katinka talked broken English, stirring up her words in such a way that the sentences were like Chinese puzzles; they needed to be taken apart and put together differently"; for example, "Please to make the door too," she says to Horace.[72]

In *Little Folks Astray* Horace, Prudy, Dotty and Flyaway go to Fulton Market in New York. Aunt Madge introduces them to Granny, an optimistic old woman who runs a stand in the market. Aunt Madge asks her if she is still happy when she is sick. Granny answers, "O, then, sometimes I feels bahd, not to be airnin nothin, and gets some afeard o' the poorhouse; but, bless ye, I can't help thinking the Lord'll keep me out."[73]

When Horace meets Wampum, an Indian boy, in *Captain Horace*, another dialect is introduced. "Me no hurt white folks; me bunkum Indian," says Wampum.[74] In the same book the Maine schoolboys make fun of Horace's Indiana accent and words: "He calls a pail a bucket, and a dipper a tin-kup" and "How he rolls his r's!"[75]

These ungrammatical, misspelled dialects, baby talk, and regionalisms are prevalent in one form or another throughout Rebecca Clarke's works. In a letter to her publishers Miss Clarke said: "I suppose you think baby talk is my mother-tongue and it would be hard work for me to write in words of two syllables but it is not so: the reverse is true. It may be I am singular in this respect, but I work harder by far over Prudies and Dimples than over any other sort of writing."[76]

These three elements—the correction of children's misbehavior, religion, and the use of baby-talk and dialects—show how Rebecca Clarke's work and effort resulted in an amazingly realistic portrayal of children. Throughout her work there is recognition of the fact that children cannot be expected to do or understand too much too soon, and a recognition that children need time to grow. In the infant stage, Flaxie doesn't understand why her fingers were snipped, so other ways to control her are used. The Parlins anxiously wait for Dotty's "reasons" to grow so that her behavior will improve. Flyaway's "baby-mischief" was humorous because she was too young to listen to her "soul-voice" tell her right from wrong. Uncle Rufus recognizes that the four-year-old twins are too young to understand God fully. Dotty interprets a Bible verse literally, and sets fire to Prudy while enacting it. Parents recognize that these children are too young to attend church or Sunday school. When some type of control is needed, physical restraint is used, because the children aren't ready yet for rational reasoning.

As the characters enter and progress through the junior stage, their understanding improves. Children are expected to attend church services and Sunday school. Furthermore, they are expected to behave and pay attention. As their "soul-voice" strengthens, their behavior begins to improve. But, as Aunt Madge says, they do not become good immediately. Instead, they progress one step at a time. As a child, Aunt Madge quits telling lies. Dotty doesn't run away again. Horace stops blowing gunpowder. But there is still plenty of other mischief to keep them occupied. Adults begin to work seriously to develop the child's conscience. First, they use stories to illustrate an appropriate moral, as with Dotty and Flaxie. Later, it is sufficient for the mother to guide a general discussion with appropriate questions. Finally, the child begins to correct his own behavior. Through this stage, the child's conceptual understanding of things improves.

By the time a child reaches the adolescent stage, he is almost an adult. There are no grammatical or conceptual problems. With a few exceptions, behavior in church or Sunday school is above reproach. An active and mature conscience and established behavior patterns keep these children out of mischief. However, it is recognized that they are not yet adults. Horace still needs guidance from his Aunt Madge. Kyzie is not yet ready to assume full responsibility for the family; Flaxie is not given the authority to punish Ethel. But they have almost developed the intellectual and behavioral patterns they will need as adults. They only require a little more time.

The portrayal of children in these three stages of development is similar in many ways to the recognized learning theories of today. Gagne developed a hierarchy of eight forms of learning. Piaget describes four stages in the development of children's learning patterns. Many writers in learning theory and educational psychology recognize developmental stages in the child. They indicate that a child needs time and experience to progress from one level to the next. Rebecca Clarke seems to have believed or sensed this, too.

Several sources indicate that real children were the models for Rebecca Clarke's fictional children. There are indications that she knew how to talk to and make friends with children. This ability undoubtedly helped her in her writing, since she never had children of her own. An unknown writer introduces an article on Rebecca Clarke by recalling her own experiences with Miss Clarke's books. "I recall my grandmother's tone as she interrupted the reading (which she enjoyed as much as did the little girls) to remark 'Now isn't that just like children.' I wondered, sometimes, why she should sound surprised. I know, now, that the children in the rare children's books of her childhood were not in the least like the real article for our Sophie May was one of the pioneers in writing children's books about real children."[77]

REFERENCES

1. "Lee and Shepard, Boston," *American Literary Gazette and Publishers Circular* 17:150, July 15, 1871.

2. Higginson, Thomas, "Children's Books of the Year," *The North American Review* 102:243, Jan. 1866.

3. Danforth, Florence, "Sophie May (Rebecca S. Clarke)." In Maine Writers Research Club. *Just Maine Folks.* Lewiston, Maine, Journal Printshop, 1924, p. 146.

4. Clarke to Lee and Shepard, Jan. 16, 1885. Quoted in Raymond L. Kilgour. *Lee and Shepard: Publishers for the People.* (Hamden, Conn.), Shoe String Press, 1965, pp. 225-26.

5. Clarke to Lee and Shepard, Sept. 1867. Quoted in Kilgour, op. cit., p. 71.

6. Clarke to Lee and Shepard, Dec. 1868. Quoted in Kilgour, op. cit., pp. 87-88.

7. Clarke to Lee and Shepard, Sept. 1867. Quoted in Kilgour, op. cit., p. 70.

8. Clarke to Lee and Shepard, Sept. 1869. Quoted in Kilgour, op. cit., p. 88.

9. Clarke to Lee and Shepard, May 1870. Quoted in Kilgour, op. cit., p. 88.

10. Abbott, John S.C. *The Mother at Home; or the Principles of Maternal Duty Familiarly Illustrated.* New York, American Tract Society, 1833. Quoted in Philip J. Greven, Jr. *Child-Rearing Concepts, 1628-1861: Historical Sources.* Itasca, Ill., F.E. Peacock, 1973, p. 122.

11. Bushnell, Horace. *Christian Nurture.* New York, Charles Scribner, 1867. Quoted in Greven, op. cit., p. 179.

12. Macleod, Anne. *A Moral Tale: Children's Fiction and American Culture, 1820-1860.* Hamden, Conn., Archon Books, 1975, p. 79.

13. Clarke, Rebecca S. *Aunt Madge's Story.* Boston, Lee and Shepard, 1872, p. 115.

14. _____ . *Dotty Dimple at Home.* Boston, Lothrop, Lee and Shepard, 1909, p. 10.

15. _____ , *Aunt Madge's Story,* op. cit., p. 19.

16. _____ . *Flaxie Frizzle.* Boston, Lee and Shepard, 1876, p. 115.

17. _____ . *Doctor Papa.* Boston, Lee and Shepard, 1877, p. 63.

18. _____ . *The Twin Cousins.* Boston, Lee and Shepard, 1880, p. 46.

19. _____ . *Wee Lucy's Secret.* Boston, Lee and Shepard, 1899, p. 147.

20. _____ . *Dotty Dimple at Play.* Boston, Lee and Shepard, 1896, pp. 72-133.

21. _____ . *Jimmy Boy.* Boston, Lee and Shepard, 1895, p. 19.

22. _____ . *Little Prudy's Captain Horace.* Chicago, M.A. Donohue, n.d., p. 24.

23. Ibid., p. 155.

24. _____ . *Prudy Keeping House.* Boston, Lee and Shepard, 1871, p. 33.

25. _____ . *Flaxie Growing Up.* Boston, Lee and Shepard, 1885, p. 18.

26. _____ . *Kyzie Dunlee, "A Golden Girl."* Boston, Lee and Shepard, 1895, p. 89.

27. Ibid., p. 116.

28. _____ , *Flaxie Growing Up,* op. cit., p. 180.

29. _____ , *Dotty Dimple at Play,* op. cit., p. 86.

30. _____ , *Flaxie Growing Up,* op. cit., p. 153.

31. _____ , *Captain Horace,* op. cit., p. 90.

32. _____ , *Doctor Papa,* op. cit., p. 145.

33. _____ , *Flaxie Growing Up,* op. cit., p. 63.

34. Ibid., p. 70.

35. "Lee and Shepard, Boston," op., cit., p. 149.

36. "New Publications," *The Catholic World* 9:429, June 1969.

37. "Rebecca Sophia Clarke." In *Dictionary of American Biography.* New York, Charles Scribner's Sons, 1943, vol. 4, p. 161.

38. "Recent Literature," *Atlantic Monthly* 43:124, Jan. 1879.

39. Clarke, *Prudy Keeping House,* op. cit., p. 93.

40. —————. *Little Prudy's Cousin Grace.* Boston, Lee and Shepard, n.d., p.17.

41. —————. *Little Prudy.* Chicago, M.A. Donohue, n.d., p. 135.

42. —————, *Captain Horace,* op. cit., p. 90.

43. —————. *Little Pitchers.* Boston, Lothop, Lee and Shepard, n.d.

44. Wood, Henrietta D. "Rebecca S. Clarke (Sophie May)," *Maine Library Bulletin,* Jan. 1929, pp. 99-100.

45. Clarke, Rebecca S. *Little Prudy's Dotty Dimple.* New York, Hurst, n.d., p. 48.

46. —————. *Dotty Dimple at Her Grandmother's.* Boston, Lee and Shepard, 1874, p. 10.

47. —————. *Kittyleen.* Boston, Lee and Shepard, 1893, p. 109.

48. —————, *Flaxie Growing Up,* op. cit., pp. 82-83.

49. —————, *Kyzie Dunlee,* op. cit., pp. 150-69.

50. Clarke to Lee and Shepard, March 24, 1864. Quoted *in* Kilgour, op. cit., p. 42.

51. Wood, op. cit., p. 101.

52. "Literature for Children," *Nation* 5:475, Dec. 12, 1867.

53. "Recent Literature," op. cit.

54. Hewins, Caroline M. "Book Reviews, Book Lists, and Articles on Children's Reading: Are They of Practical Value to the Children's Librarian?" *Library Journal* 26:59, Aug. 1901.

55. Clarke, *Flaxie Frizzle,* op. cit., p. 10.

56. Ibid., pp. 13-14.

57. —————. *Wee Lucy: Little Prudy's "Wee Croodlin' Doo."* Boston, Lee and Shepard, 1894, pp. 51-52.

58. —————, *Wee Lucy's Secret,* op. cit., p. 45.

59. —————, *Little Prudy's Dotty Dimple,* op. cit., p. 85.

60. —————. *Dotty Dimple's Flyaway.* Boston, Lee and Shepard, 1870, p. 22.

61. —————, *Cousin Grace,* op. cit., p. 151.

62. —————, *Dotty Dimple at Her Grandmother's,* op. cit., p. 79.

63. —————, *Little Prudy's Dotty Dimple,* op. cit., pp. 40-41.

64. —————, *Wee Lucy's Secret,* op. cit., pp. 111-12.

65. —————, *Doctor Papa,* op. cit., pp. 168-69.

66. —————, *Twin Cousins,* op. cit., pp. 110-11.

67. —————, *Jimmy Boy,* op. cit., p. 23.

68. —————, *Kyzie Dunlee,* op. cit., p. 50.

69. —————, *Wee Lucy,* op. cit., p. 22.

70. —————, *Cousin Grace,* op. cit., p. 108.

71. Ibid., p. 49.

72. —————. *Dotty Dimple Out West.* Boston, Lee and Shepard, 1874, pp. 90-91.

73. —————. *Little Folks Astray.* Boston, Lee and Shepard, 1871, p. 175.

74. —————, *Captain Horace,* op. cit., p. 138.

75. Ibid., p. 66.

76. Clarke to Lee and Shepard, Sept. 1869. Quoted *in* Kilgour, op. cit., p. 88.

77. "Sophie May (Rebecca S. Clarke; 1833-1906)," *Maine Library Bulletin,* Jan. 1929, p. 97.

V—VIRGINIE ARROSE SES VIOLETTES
CHAQUE MATIN ET CHAQUE SOIR.

First Appearances:
Literature in Nineteenth-Century
Periodicals for Children

HARRIETT R. CHRISTY

Walter Library, which is on the mall of the University of Minnesota-Minneapolis campus, near the east bank of the Mississippi River, has at the end of one of its corridors a dark, wood-paneled room with signs of the zodiac painted on the oak beams of its ceiling. Bells gently announce your arrival as you open the door to the quiet of solid oak tables, subdued light, and walls lined with shelves of books. This room, the reading room for the Children's Literature Research Collections, is a place of retreat—retreat to the world of children's literature, both past and present—and a place for scholarly study of the many forms and dimensions that literature represents.

The Children's Literature Research Collections embodies several different collections and contains about 31,000 books; 1600 manuscripts; illustrations for 2400 books; 2000 comic books and Big-Little books; 10,000 series books for boys and girls; 70,000 dime novels and story papers; a special collection of Paul Bunyan folklore; the Wanda Gág collection of original manuscripts and books; the Bertha Rudolph collection of wall hangings, figurines, and bookmarks related to children's literature; and approximately 45 long shelves of nineteenth- and twentieth-century children's periodicals.

The private collections of two men formed the initial core of this research collection. Dr. Irvin Kerlan, a native Minnesotan who was chief of medical research for the Food and Drug Administration in Washington, D.C., collected rare books. One day a friend gave him a copy of Friskey's *Johnny Cottontail,* then a new children's book. Whatever its charm was, Dr. Kerlan had embarked on a new direction in his hobby. His interest in how a book grew in the mind of an author or illustrator led him to request evidence of the creative process. The authors and illustrators responded to his interest by sending him their original manuscripts, art work, dummies of the completed book, and, sometimes, an inscribed copy of the first edition. By 1949 Dr. Kerlan saw the need for a permanent home for the materials filling his house. Although many institutions wished to obtain his collection, an agreement was reached with the University of Minnesota, establishing the Kerlan Collection there and giving him the acclaim he so thoroughly enjoyed.

The second man, whose hobby became part of the Children's Literature Research Collections in 1954, was George Hess. He was a railway executive who had read nickel and dime novels as a boy. In 1928 he began collecting the novels, hoping to find copies that had once belonged to him. His search led to a collection of almost 50,000 dime novels, story papers, and pulps, but not one had his name on it. Nearly every title published is represented; however, there are gaps in individual titles.

The original manuscripts and illustrations, which are housed between acid-free papers under climate-controlled conditions, will be of particular interest to some researchers. Many titles have a complete set of materials from the inital sketch or note, through the galley proofs and final draft for publication, to a copy of the book inscribed by the author or illustrator (often giving a clue as to why the book was written). Influences on the creative process can be observed from margin notes made by both editor and creator. The goal of this segment of the Children's Literature Research Collections, as expressed by Dr. Karen Nelson Hoyle, the curator, is to acquire complete sets for in-depth research of a single book, a single author, or a single illustrator.

Children's periodicals comprise another large segment of the collection. There are approximately 150 titles of both English and American magazines. Some are complete (*Harper's Young People, Oliver Optic's* magazines. Some are complete (*Harper's Young People, Oliver Optic's Magazine, Riverside Magazine, Wide Awake, Our Young Folks*); some are almost complete (*Youth's Companion, Youth's Casket, Student and Schoolmate, Juvenile Miscellany*); others have gaps of varying degrees. The majority of the magazines are American, secular, and from the nineteenth century.

There is no subject index for the Children's Literature Research Collections. Access, however, is possible in several different ways—by author, by illustrator, by manuscript or illustration, by language, or by chronology. A separate card catalog lists series books, dime novels, comic books, periodicals, and the Paul Bunyan folklore. Original materials are filed alphabetically by contributor, with an annotation describing the extent and type of material (notes, drawings, jacket layout, correspondence, etc.). Books dating from 1717 to 1925 are listed in the chronological file. Forty-six languages are represented in the 4000 books, which are cataloged first by language, then alphabetically by author within that language.

To know the basic purpose of the collection is to know and respect the rules set up for the preservation and use of any unique and irreplaceable materials. Therefore, the collection is noncirculating, assuring a researcher that the material wanted is always available. Children may come to the collection on field trips with a teacher or librarian. Answering reference questions by mail, exhibits, fellowships, sponsorship of authors and illustrators for speeches—these are some of the other activities of the Children's Literature Research Collections staff.

Before discussing the research design, a word needs to be clarified and defined. In using the word *classic*, or in referring to "the classics," I imply no judgment or criticism of the literature, its author, or the times from which it arose. Through the years adults have compiled lists of books children should read and have called them by various names—Books to be Remembered, Old Favorites, Books Too Good to Miss, Lasting Favorites, or, simply, Classics. Discerning readers had found the literature appealing, but someone else, not I, determined that the literature be placed on a list. This is the only basis on which I call the literature "classic."

Now for a brief look at the research process and design. While searching for a topic for a final paper in Dr. Harris McClaskey's History of Children's Literature course, I can remember coming across the words *annual* and *keepsake*. What were they? Who published them? Who wrote for them? When? For whom were they intended? From these questions I was gently led into the world of nineteenth-century children's periodicals, and I was trapped. Besides a paper for the course, my interest led to a master's paper, and to an independent study which resulted in the presentation of slides of "first appearances" of the classics.

The steps in the research process can be identified as follows:

1. making the literature search
   a. *Library Literature*
   b. *Dissertation Abstracts*
   c. Master's Theses
2. reading the secondary sources
   a. Meigs's *Critical History of Children's Literature*
   b. adult magazine articles of the late nineteenth and early twentieth centuries
   c. dissertations (Lyons, Merrill, Erisman)
   d. surveys of American literature
3. compiling a bibliography for further reading from the secondary sources
4. using interlibrary loan and the University of Minnesota archives to secure dissertations and books not available locally
5. compiling a list of classics first published in a magazine
6. verifying periodical title, publication place, and date
   a. *Union List of Serials*
   b. Mott—*History of American Magazines*
7. verifying publication date of literature
   a. biographies of individual authors
   b. histories of publishing houses
   c. *National Union Catalog of pre-1956 Imprints*
   d. *U.S. Catalog*
   e. *Cumulative Book Index*
8. examining lists of classics by Hewins, Anne Moore, Montrose Moses, Bertha Mahoney, Frances Olcott, and others
9. locating the literature on the page of the magazine (searching the primary sources); deciding what to film; arranging for the photographer
10. ordering one slide from the University of Texas-Denton for the only example not available at the Children's Literature Research Collections

As with most research, some problems were encountered. None of them were insurmountable, however. For example, secondary sources did not always distinguish magazines published in America from those published in England. Not all magazines have an index, or at least one that was bound in. Sometimes this meant going through a bound volume page by page to locate an item. Often the year of the book publication given in the *U.S. Catalog* or the *pre-1956 Imprints* was the same as the magazine publication date, when, in fact, the literature did appear in the magazine first. In later years the magazine date became the copyright date. Fourth, biographies of authors and histories of publishing houses seldom, if ever, mention writing or publishing for children. The cover and title pages of a magazine occasionally were not included when single issues were bound into the annual volume. This created difficulty in verifying dates, since early magazines did not print the date on inside pages as is now done. Volumes were physically moved from one library to another while research was in progress.

As I began to think about the best way to present the research results within the framework of the topic for this symposium, I considered several different approaches. First, I tried to fit all the examples into the pattern suggested by R. Gordon Kelly in *Mother Was a Lady*, i.e., that children's fiction issued from and reinforced the gentry of America—the ladies and gentlemen of the drawing room rather than the men and women of the farm, factory or frontier. But several examples did not fit that pattern.

Next, I tried to fit them into the three periods of children's magazines: (1) 1789-1840, the period of didacticism, with religious themes dominating the writing; (2) 1840-60, when there was less emphasis on morality and religion and more emphasis on sentimentality, materialism and escapism; (3) post-Civil War, when reading for the enjoyment of reading predominated, still with its emphasis on proper living, however. But that was rather like the Indian fable of the blind men and the elephant. To see one part is not to see the whole. To isolate one story to prove a point is to ignore the other types of material printed during the same period.

Then I tried to outguess the publishers. Did they have a divine insight to know which magazine serial to publish in book form and which not to? What about those hundreds of serials and books which were published but never became "classics"? And what about the classics? Is there an inherent quality which assures them automatic and long-lasting success and readability? That is a question which is not going to be resolved in the very near future.

What about the children—the ones who read the magazines at night by the light of a candle or a rag burning in a bowl of lard? Researchers agree that the child had little or nothing to say about what was published in the magazines. Ministers and mothers, it seems, knew best what children should read. What would the child of the nineteenth century have put on his/her list of classics? Would it resemble the list adults prepared? Would the children even have had the prerogative to make such a list? Were the children in the stories examples that the children themselves would choose for their ideals and heroes? I cannot answer those questions.

I also considered editorial control. Did restrictions influence the literature? Certainly, formulas were recommended by editors and followed by authors. But is this really why we find Frank Stockton's *Floating Prince*, Palmer Cox's *Brownies*, or Kipling's *Just-So Stories* on classics lists?

What about the work ethic? How much does that affect the literature for children in the nineteenth century?

Since these approaches seemed to be inadequate, and would be doing what I did not intend originally, I decided to consider the slides simply for what they are: examples of children's literature in their pre-book form. What distinguishes these examples from all the other literature of the nineteenth century is the simple fact that they appeared first in a magazine, later in book form, and still later on lists of books recommended by adults for children to read. This, then, is the way the classic looked on the pages of the magazine in the 1800s. These are the "first appearances."

The year was 1789. In France, rebellion against Louis XVI resulted in the storming of the Bastille and the beginning of the French Revolution. Hannah More and her sisters had recently established their first Sunday school in Cheddar, England, in order to counteract the threat of atheism spreading across the country and to teach the ragged children of the downtrodden to read. Far across the seas in "America," thirteen Atlantic seaboard colonies, after fighting to free themselves from European domination, united under a constitution and called on George Washington to be their first leader.

Life, whether in France, England or America, was harsh, cruel and demanding. There was little time for pleasure or fun. A family struggling to provide daily food, clothing and shelter for themselves found little time for intellectual or aesthetic pursuits. Children as well as adults knew the necessity of working hard in order to survive. They worked beside their elders on the farm, in the home, and in the shop, and were treated by their parents as ignorant men and women, not as persons worthy of being developed. As a result, children were expected to learn to read the same heavy literary fare that was available to the adults. Writers were apologetic for even wasting their time on such efforts as books of instruction in religious affairs or books of morals and manners. Children, after all, were to learn "not to live, but to dye" and their books taught them to do so in a proper manner.

Within this framework of severity and repression, the year 1789 becomes significant in the history of children's literature in America. At a time when the population of the colonies numbered only 5.5 million (equal to the current number of our unemployed people), two publishers began a venture which was to set the stage for developments and influences that continue to the present day. The event was the publication in Hartford, Connecticut, of a periodical appropriately called *The Children's Magazine*. It was the first such periodical in America intended to appeal to the interests of a specific group of people—children. The stated intent of the publishers was:

> To furnish Children, from seven to twelve years of age, with a variety of lessons on various subjects, written in a plain, neat, familiar style, and proper to lead them from the easy language of the Spelling-Books up to the more difficult style of the best writers. Teachers of School have long complained of the want of such a work, and the Publishers are happy that they are now enabled to furnish it at a small expense.[1]

Barzallai Hudson and George Goodwin combined the most desirable features of the small-sized *New England Primer* and the popular chapbooks and hoped to provide instruction, morality, and some measure of amusement through the "good," "wholesome" characters in their stories.

Even though the first magazine for children was published so long ago, children's periodicals are often disregarded in the history of American children's literature. Yet many of the stories and poems included on lists of classics for children appeared first in a magazine before being published in book form. Children had various types of periodicals to read throughout the century. There were Sunday school tracts, blood-and-thunders, weeklies, story papers, school magazines, and publications with special causes such as temperance. But it was primarily in the magazine published for home reading that we find the literature later considered classic. Editors and publishers, both wise and fortunate, chose from the vast amount of material written for the pages of these magazines what they thought would sell and continue to be read, and published it in book form.

Who, then, were the authors who dared not only to write for children but also to be published first in a magazine? And what was it that later became known as a classic? Probably the earliest known classic to be found in a children's periodical is William Cullen Bryant's "To a Fringed Gentian." It appeared in the November 1828 issue of *Juvenile Miscellany*, which was designed for the "instruction and amusement of youth," according to its editor, Lydia Child. The magazine carried moralistic, didactic stories as well as conundrums, puzzles, riddles, and lessons in natural philosophy (many of the same features found in magazines of today). The variety of departments exemplified the fact that someone already recognized that the child had a mind that might be developed in a variety of ways.

Strong abolitionist views forced Lydia Maria Child to give up the editorship of *Juvenile Miscellany* in 1834, and Sarah Josepha Hale, it is believed, then became editor. While Sarah Hale is best known as the editor for forty years of *Godey's Lady's Book*, the magazine for women that offered the latest in fashions, etiquette and recipes, she is also remembered for the second classic found in a children's periodical— "Mary's Lamb" (*Juvenile Miscellany*, September-October 1830).

Several years later *Little Pilgrim* introduced John Greenleaf Whittier's "Barefoot Boy" to young readers (January 1855). Here was a boy, not of the gentry class but of the common, rural folk, a barefoot boy celebrating the outdoors. Some have said this is a sign that the democratic movement found an outlet even in literature for children. Sarah Lippincott, using the name Grace Greenwood, edited the magazine which had on its cover the picture of a little pilgrim child, staff in hand, trudging through life's vicissitudes. On its inside pages were vivid fictional accounts of brave, hardy, determined Christian boys and girls. The editor, in the first issue in January 1854, addressed the child readers in this way:

> Are you not all charmed and delighted dear readers, with our new heading? Was there ever in the world, think you, so comely a little pilgrim as Mr. Darley has sketched for us?...The freshness and youth of his round, sunny face, must win quick responses from the freshness and youth of your generous hearts; and his sweet, wondering eyes draw tender, loving looks from yours—especially YOURS, ye little maidens. Is he not beautiful to behold?

The editor also stated in the prospectus of volume 1, number 2 (February 1854):

> It is not our intention to discuss profound religious doctrines or political problems with our young readers. But while we urge upon them no peculiar sectarian views, our aim shall always be to inculcate a high religious morality....It will be our object not only to adapt our paper to the tastes and comprehension of children, but to render it pleasant reading for parents and teachers.

One of the inducements for subscribing to the magazine was that almost all the material was original. Moreover, *Little Pilgrim* contained more matter for fifty cents than many of the juvenile publications for a dollar, so said the editor.

The population of America had reached 25 million when *Student and Schoolmate Magazine* (1855-72) carried the very first Horatio Alger story—"Ragged Dick." Written and serialized in 1867, the story paralleled a significant change in social thinking of the time: anyone willing to work could raise himself from rags to riches. Children were now learning that the middle-class Protestant values of piety and meekness could be replaced by competition and aggressiveness. Gradually the work ethic with its increased emphasis on materialism would become a new source of subject matter in literature for young readers.

The intent of the editors, as stated in the November 1855 issue, was somewhat different from that of the previous periodicals:

> What better name could be chosen? Every student likes to have a schoolmate and all schoolmates should be good students....Here the reader will find interesting articles on philosophy, history, astronomy, geography, natural history, travels, and other branches of study, illustrated with beautiful engravings....Its aims are EXCELSIOR, awakening noble aspirations in the minds of youth, and ever pointing them to something higher and better. It goes forth, not merely to beguile the passing hour, but with a higher object—to instruct....Besides, it will, unlike the usual class-books, be read during vacations as well as in school months....Reader, whoever you may be, whether teacher, pupil, parent, boy, or girl, you have an interest in this work; for he that has a heart and keeps it, a mind that hungers and supplies it, who seeks a useful and not a worthless life, will find encouragement and assistance here.

By now free public education was no longer a privilege of wealthy people, although many children continued to work long hours in factories or on farms. Whereas European children learned to know their place in the world, American children had to make their place. Frontier life had developed a rigorous independence in each person and this influenced child rearing attitudes. Likewise, the institutions of society were challenged to new responsibilities as a result of secularization and weakening of the family unit, urbanization, westward migration, and mechanization. The challenge was reflected in the literature for children.

Familiar because of its bright orange cover and called by some researchers the first modern children's periodical, *Our Young Folks* (1855-74) introduced several classics to its young readers. The editors, Gail Hamilton, John Trowbridge and Lucy Larcom, believed their magazine would uplift the hearts of their readers. They believed, too, that reading could be for fun and not just to acquire information or to form character. Children were to see and enjoy nature through exercise, gardening and games. Work would bring happiness and its own reward, they maintained.

In February 1865 *Our Young Folks* published Celia Thaxter's poem, "The Sandpiper"; in following months it also published her less well-known "Chanticleer," "Albatross," and "Cockatoos." Charles Dickens, who had been writing for children's periodicals in England, became known to readers of *Our Young Folks* in 1867 with his "Holiday Romance." This light, whimsical story with a fairy-tale quality is an early example of a make-believe story within a longer story; it is known to us as *The Magic Fishbone*. (How unlike a book published that same year—the first Elsie Dinsmore story!)

The periodical continued its publication of classics-to-be by serializing Thomas Bailey Aldrich's *Story of a Bad Boy* (1869). Aldrich wrote of his own boyhood in Portsmouth (called Rivermouth in the story), depicting a boy as he really was and not as his elders thought he ought to be. Tom was more than an inherently evil boy; he was a person. And Aldrich was an author who was brave enough to admit that Tom might rather use his pennies to buy bull's-eye marbles than to help the missionaries convert the heathens in far-off places.

Meanwhile, girls were enchanted by the simplistic family stories of Little Prudy and Dotty Dimple written in 1867, 1868, and 1869 by Rebecca Clarke, using the name Sophie May. Although lists of classics compiled by librarians and educators may not have included these stories, it is quite certain that lists made by girls would have. Without a doubt, Little Prudy and Dotty Dimple helped increase readership of not only the magazine but also the books which were subsequently published.

In 1870, three years after Dickens's "Holiday Romance" was published in America, another English writer, Edward Lear, had a now-famous poem printed in *Our Young Folks*—"The Owl and the Pussycat." His serious but funny play on words and the equally playful illustrations must have delighted, and may even have puzzled, the child reared by the strict morality of the McGuffey Readers.

Reading for pleasure and recreation was being accepted as right and desirable. The ulterior motives of satisfying a thirst for information and inculcating moral values no longer strictly bound editors, publishers and authors. Children were increasingly being recognized as persons rather than as miniature adults. Education for everyone, accelerated industrialization, westward expansion, and better forms of communication contributed to changing lifestyles in which there was leisure time to read. It was not difficult, within this changing climate, for Horace Scudder to find readers for two sets of stories that appeared first in the magazine he edited, *Riverside Magazine*: the Ting-a-Ling stories by Frank Stockton and the eleven original and six translated fairy tales by Hans Christian Andersen. The titles (e.g., *Chicken Grethe, The Most Extraordinary Thing, The Great Grandfather, The Candles*) are not the most familiar ones, but they are a sign that imaginative literature was indeed beginning to take its place as a legitimate genre in America; authors would find a growing market for literature of the imagination.

During the four years of its life, 1867-70, *Riverside Magazine* reached a high standard of quality for children's periodicals. Scudder was determined to develop a critical attitude toward books and reading matter for young people. In a January 1867 column called "Books for Young People," he states:

> It may seem suicidal, but we begin this series of informal notes, intended for children's elders, with the remark that children have too much reading nowadays....A literature is forming which is destined to act powerfully upon general letters....The time must soon come when students of literature must consider the character and tendency of CHILDREN'S LETTERS....Children have too much reading, and the fault is not theirs but their elders'....The modern magazine offers a great relief to the overburdened reader, by making him, with great economy, familiar with the latest subject that is talked about....It is one step toward the simple system of choosing our constant reading matter from what is best in literature, and not necessarily from what is latest, though some still seem to think that books, like breakfast-cakes, are good only when hot....Magazines for young people have this in their favor, that they are substitutes for many books; the freshest and most enjoyable literature can be given there in compact form, with all the seduction of an expected weekly or monthly arrival, and so that hunger for mere reading, which they share with their elders, can be appeased at no great cost of time and attention....If we select for children with real care, there will always be a check upon idle reading; but if we let them gather what they like from Sunday-school, day-school, and public libraries, and only cast our eyes over the books to see that they have no wicked-looking words in them, we may expect to see them grow up listless readers, with a taste spoiled for the richest and finest literature by being satiated with leanness.

As editor of books for the Houghton Publishing Company, Horace Scudder's influence was to continue for many years after *Riverside Magazine* ceased publication.

Wide Awake Magazine (1875-93), intended for ten- to eighteen-year-old readers, carried illustrations of various sizes, complete music lessons (suggesting a degree of affluence which allowed a family to have a piano or organ in the home), lessons in cookery, early stories by George Mac-Donald, and supplements for the Chautauqua Young Folks Reading Union sponsored by the then-popular Chautauqua movement. The magazine is remembered also for the first publication, in serialized form, of the antics of the Five Little Peppers. Margaret Sidney designed her lively Pepper family so that children of all ages and generations would enjoy stories about them. Adding character to both the author and the magazine, and interest for the child reader, an author's hand-written signature accompanied many of the stories in *Wide Awake*.

By 1880 the population of the United States had reached 50 million; by 1900 it would reach 76 million. An illustrated weekly magazine published for twenty years just before the turn of the century (1879-99), *Harper's Young People*, was most notable for the introduction of Howard Pyle to children. Often considered the best retelling of the Robin Hood stories, Pyle's *Merry Adventures of Robin Hood* began without fanfare or illustration on page 147 of volume 4 in 1883. Several of his fairy stories were also tested first by magazine publication. "The Bird in the Linden Tree," "The Apple of Contentment," "Dame Margery," and "Claus and His Wonderful Staff" all became part of *Pepper and Salt*, published in book form in 1885. "King Stork" and "The Swan Maiden" were among those tales children read first in *Harper's Young People* and later in the book called *Wonder Clock* (1887).

Two other classics were first published by *Harper's Young People*. *Toby Tyler...or Ten Years with a Circus* was written by James Otis in 1880; *A Boy's Town* (1890) by William Dean Howells described Howells's life as a boy in Hamilton, Ohio, and is still regarded as a good picture of frontier life in the early 1800s.

When the subject of nineteenth-century children's periodicals is mentioned, probably the magazine first to be recalled is *St. Nicholas*. Although its life (1873-1940) was not as long as that of *Youth's Companion* (1827-1929), it was able to gain a greater stature because of a combination of circumstances. Scribner's Publishing Company had absorbed several prominent children's periodicals (*Our Young Folks, Little Corporal, Children's Hour, School-day Magazine, Wide Awake*) with their lists of subscribers and the most desirable features of each. More importantly, it secured Mary Mapes Dodge as its editor. Dodge knew authors and illustrators, understood children, and was able to convince authors and illustrators they should write and draw particularly for children. Scribner's was willing to pay the authors and illustrators for their work, and the result was a long list of first appearances in the magazine. In July 1873 Mary Mapes Dodge wrote an article for *Scribner's Monthly* in which she deplored the state of periodicals for children, claiming that harm was being done by nearly all that were published. "We edit for the approval of fathers and mothers, and endeavor to make the child's monthly a milk-and-water variety of the adult's periodical. But, in fact, the child's magazine needs to be stronger, truer, bolder, more uncompromising than the other."[2] She wanted no sermonizing; her magazine should be strong, warm, beautiful, true, with moral teaching done by hint only. Children could find for themselves joy and pleasure in stars *and* daisies, she thought. Pictures with variety, simplicity, beauty, and unity would help make the magazine the child's own pleasure ground. Her authors were not required to write either up or down to children. Imaginative, informative, illustrated stories could be written purely for a child's delight. Writing·talent, combined with tact and intuition, was at long last respectable.

Louisa Alcott, already known for *Little Women*, and *Eight Cousins* serialized in *St. Nicholas* in 1875, *Under the Lilacs* in 1877, had *Jack and Jill* in 1879. Children and parents whose own lives were not far removed from frontier experiences could read *Boy Emigrants* (Noah Brooks, 1875-76). This preceded Howells's account (in *Harper's Young People*) and is also an excellent, accurate picture of life on the frontier. Edward Eggleston, writing about the harsh treatment he received in rural schools of Indiana, wrote *Hoosier Schoolboy* for *St. Nicholas* in 1881-182. Charles Carryl wrote his marvelously imaginative *Davy and the Goblin; or, What Followed Reading Alice's Adventures in Wonderland* for serialization in 1884-85. The "Sugar Plum Garden," Butterscotchmen, Rigsby, and The Whale in a Waistcoat deserve to be storybook friends of children today. Xerox Corporation thought so, too, and published a new edition of the book in 1967.

Although Frank Stockton was assistant editor to Dodge from 1873-1881, he still found time to write his own tales for the imagination of children. In 1880 "Floating Prince" appeared in *St. Nicholas*. "Bee-Man and His Original Form" (later to be known as *The Bee-Man of Orn*) was illustrated by E.B. Bensell and published in 1883. And in 1885 a tale which still captures the imagination of storytellers, listeners and illustrators became a permanent record in *St. Nicholas*—"The Griffin and the Minor Canon."

It is a long way from the world of the tricky sprites and amusing goblins of Frank Stockton to the hero of the next classic published in a children's periodical. With *Little Lord Fauntleroy* (1885-86), Frances Burnett as author and Reginald Birch as illustrator immortalized a type of clothing as well as a type of personality for young boys. A second story, "Sara Crewe; or What Happened at Miss Minchin's" (1887-88), was so popular in the magazine that she made it into a play. That, in turn, was so well received that Burnett expanded the story into the book we know as *The Little Princess.*

Between 1879 and 1886 the antics of hundreds of Brownies were introduced to *St. Nicholas* readers by Palmer Cox. Imagine the fun a child must have had following the capers of the Dude, the Cowboy, the Jockey, or the Policeman from one issue of the magazine to the next. The works of the famous naturalist, Ernest E. Thompson (also known as Ernest

Thompson-Seton), are represented by short essays about animals, with drawings that identify their features and illustrate their tracks and habitat. "Tracks in the Snow" (1885), "Drummer on Snowshoes" (1887), and "Screech Owl" (1890) later became part of a book of collected nature studies.

Readers who had surreptitiously enjoyed Mark Twain's adventures of Tom Sawyer and Huck Finn were not likely to miss "Tom Sawyer Abroad" when it was published in *St. Nicholas* in 1893-94. The November 1896 issue carried the first chapter of a story by John Bennett—*Master Skylark.* The subsequent parts of the serial described life in sixteenth-century England. Rudyard Kipling's tales were first tested in *St. Nicholas: Toomai of the Elephants* (1893), *Potted Princess* (1893), *Tiger-Tiger* (1894), *Mowgli's Brothers* (1894), *Rikki-Tikki-Tavi* (1895), *Just-So Stories* (1897-98), and *How the Camel Got His Hump* (1898).

Entertainment was not the only motive for publication in *St. Nicholas.* Manners could be taught to children, Gelett Burgess thought, through humorous rhyme and simple drawings. Mary Mapes Dodge must have agreed with him, and so on the pages of the magazine in 1898 and 1899 we find those hairless, noseless Goops teaching about Obedience, Caution, Curiosity, Politeness, Interruption, and Bed-time. Far into the twentieth century the rhymes, then in book form, were used by parents as a palatable way to teach proper conduct.

This brings the study to the end of the nineteenth century. There are many more examples of first appearances; the research is by no means complete. But this summary shows how far the publishers and editors, the authors and illustrators, the children and their parents had come from the early magazines designed to teach the child how to cope with a harsh, cruel life. Neither the mind of the child nor that of the author needed to be compromised any longer. Children had at last become real people and authors were not afraid to sign their real names to what they wrote.

REFERENCES

1. Richardson, Lyon. *History of Early American Magazines.* New York, Octagon, 1966, p. 336.

2. Dodge, Mary Mapes. "Children's Magazines," *Scribner's Monthly,* July 1873, pp. 352-54.

W—Winifred est américaine, elle n'est pas une petite française.

SELECTED BIBLIOGRAPHY OF READINGS AND SOURCES

Addison, Daniel Dulany. *Lucy Larcom: Life, Letters, and Diary*. New York, Houghton, Mifflin, 1894.

Alstetter, M.F. "Early American Magazines for Children." *Peabody Journal of Education* 19:131-36 Nov. 1941.

Andrews, Siri, ed. *The Hewins Lectures, 1947-1962*. Boston, Horn Book, 1963.

Blum, John Morton, ed. *Yesterday's Children: An Anthology compiled from the pages of "Our Young Folks"*. Boston, Houghton, Mifflin & Co., 1959.

Chew, Samuel C., ed. *Fruit Among the Leaves*. New York, Appleton, 1950.

Davis, Sheldon Emmor. *Educational Periodicals during the Nineteenth Century*. Metuchen, N.J., Scarecrow Press, 1970

Egoff, Sheila A. *Children's Periodicals of the Nineteenth Century*. London, The Library Association, 1951.

Erisman, Fred. "There was a Child Went Forth: A Study of *St. Nicholas* Magazine and Selected Children's Authors, 1890-1915." Ph.D. diss. University of Minnesota, 1966.

Howard, Alice B. *Mary Mapes Dodge of St. Nicholas*. New York, Junior Literary Guild, 1943.

Jordan, Alice M. "Our Young Folks: Its Editors and Authors," *Horn Book* 10:348-54, Nov. 1934.

_____ . "Juvenile Miscellany," *American Journal of Education* 1:569ff, Sept. 1826.

Kelly, R. Gordon. *Mother Was a Lady: Self and Society in Selected American Children's Periodicals, 1865-1890*. Westport, Conn., Greenwood Press, 1974.

Kuhn, Anne. *The Mother's Role in Childhood Education: New England Concepts 1830-1860*. New Haven, Conn., Yale University Press, 1947.

Lyon, Betty L. "A History of Children's Secular Magazines Published in the United States from 1789 to 1899." Ph.D. diss. Johns Hopkins University, 1942.

Macleod, Anne Scott. *A Moral Tale: Children's Fiction and American Culture, 1820-1860*. New York, Shoe String Press, 1975.

Matthews, Harriet L. "Magazines for Children," *Bulletin of Bibliography* 1:133-36, April 1899.

Meigs, Cornelia, et al. *A Critical History of Children's Literature.* New York, Macmillan,, 1969.

Merrill, Goldie P. "The Development of American Secular Juvenile Magazines; A Study of the Educational Significance of their Content." Ph.D. diss. University of Washington, 1938.

Moore, Annie E. "Magazines for Children," *Elementary English Review* 14:58-60, Feb. 1937.

Nolen, Eleanor W. "Nineteenth Century Children's Magazines,"*Horn Book* 15:55-60, Jan. 1939.

Rodgers, Daniel T. *The Work Ethic in Industrial America. 1850-1920.* Chicago, University of Chicago Press, 1978.

Schiller, Justin G. "Magazines for Young America," *Columbia Library Columns* 23:24-39, May 1974.

Sturges, Florence M. "The St. Nicholas Bequest," *Horn Book* 36:365-77, Oct. 1960.

Tebbel, John. *From Rags to Riches: Horatio Alger. Jr. and the American Dream.* New York, Macmillan, 1963.

Tryon, W.S. *Parnassus Corner: A Life of James T. Fields, Publisher to the Victorians.* New York, Riverside Press, 1963.

X—XÉNOPHON EST LE GÉNÉRAL RENOMMÉ
À QUI PAUL CROIT RESSEMBLER.

Y—Y A-T-IL UNE AUTRE PETITE FILLE DE
SI JOLIS YEUX ?

Poetry for Children of Two Centuries

JOHN MACKAY SHAW

No century ends precisely at midnight December 31, but projects itself into the century that follows. The nineteenth century was especially tenacious of life because of the seemingly deathless spirit of its dominant figure, Queen Victoria. That spirit lived on in her son, Edward VII. It faded only with his death in 1910, and died four years later in the cataclysm of the First World War.

I have been interested in what this symposium might have to say about the nineteenth-century child, having myself been born when Victoria was still alive. I was one of the host of children let out of school to greet Edward and his beautiful Queen Alexandra on their triumphal coronation visit to Scotland in 1902. As a newsboy eight years later, I delivered to my neighbors the purple-bordered copies of the *Glasgow Herald* that brought them the news of his death.

My perspective of nineteenth-century children and their books is therefore that of a participant no less than as an interested observer viewing them from afar. My first exposure to books was definitely that of a nineteenth-century child, which may explain a certain bias you may detect in what I have to say.

My children and grandchildren, on the other hand, are just as definitely twentieth-century children, and since I have to some extent been involved in their upbringing, I am aware of the great gap that separates their reading and listening habits from mine. The social and technological changes since World War I have given them a much better chance for productive and enjoyable lives than was possible for me and my classmates. The doorway to knowledge has been opened much more widely before them. They have had more leisure to devote to self-improvement and to the many pleasures that flow from accomplishment in the arts, and because of the advances in the science of medicine they are likely to live much longer to enjoy them. They live in a world grown infinitely smaller in compass, so that they are in instant communication with anyone in it, and can reach any part of it in a matter of hours. Some of them will actually live and work beyond the confines of this world, provided unwise leadership does not destroy them all in the meantime.

Nonetheless I have been aware of one special area in which their environment has been inferior to the one I was brought up in. I refer to poetry, which reached its zenith in the second half of the nineteenth century, but which in the twentieth century may properly be called the neglected art. And this I consider a matter of vital importance to the future of the race, for if there is one thing of which we may be sure in this age of obfuscation, it is that poetry in the preceding ten centuries has been the channel through which each generation has transmitted its wisdom to the one that follows it. And of what value is all our knowledge if it does not walk hand in hand with wisdom? May not mankind's increasing understanding of the ways of nature be actually destructive if there be not wise minds to direct its use?

It would perhaps be wise for me to explain what I mean by poetry, for it is an art that has always had as many definitions as practitioners. Poetry shares with prose the common purpose of so arranging words that, when read inwardly or spoken aloud, thought will be conveyed as clearly as possible from one mind to another. Poetry, however, differs from prose in that whereas prose is free and untrammeled, poetry is subject to certain confining rules, the authority for which lies in the work of thousands of poets writing over a period of hundreds of years. The chief elements of these rules may be briefly described as follows:

first, a rhythmic cadence achieved through the use of regular meters; second, a melodic theme achieved through the use of such sound effects as rhyme and alliteration; and

third, a linguistic brilliance achieved through the use of such verbal images as simile and metaphor.

These three elements must be mingled in such a way that the sentences are harmoniously pleasing, the mood of the poet forcefully conveyed, his meaning clearly and emphatically expressed, and his message firmly fixed in the memory and readily repeated. When one or more of these elements is absent, the language is to that extent less poetic and more prosaic.

To those of you who majored in English at college, and especially to those of you who struggled through to a Ph.D., this definition may sound ridiculously simplistic, but I find it helpful in distinguishing the kind of poetry to which we nineteenth-century children were exposed from what is presented as poetry in the learned journals of the twentieth century.

It was this kind of clear, rhythmical, musical poetry that confronted us nineteenth-century children wherever we turned—in the home, in the school, in church, and in the periodicals that were our delight. We read it, we memorized it, we declaimed it, not always willingly, sometimes resentfully, but so constantly and in such profusion that it burned into our souls and became what Isaac Watts called the "furniture of our minds." Our teachers, whose minds were similarly furnished, made use of verse in teaching every subject in the curriculum.

When the nineteenth century began, Watt's *Divine and Moral Songs* was a standard textbook in every school in Britain and America, and was carried into the homes in every peddler's pack. Wilbur Macey Stone, an indefatigable collector of such ephemera, identified more than a thousand editions of Watts published between 1750 and 1850. Walter de la Mare wrote of it that childhood without the sluggard and the busy bee would resemble a hymnbook without "O God, our help in ages past." Its preface is a teacher's aid addressed "to all that are concerned with the education of children," and its advice is as fresh and timely as if written yesterday. Would that every student in our modern departments of education were as well advised.

Those neatly dressed urchins that we see in the old Bewick woodcuts, lined up on wooden benches, are no doubt listening to one of their classmates tremblingly intoning Watt's Song Two, "Praise for Creation and Providence." Those of you who attend church are familiar with the powerful tune to which it has been set, but how many of you are conscious of the words as you sing it?

I sing the almighty power of God
  That made the mountains rise,
That spread the flowing seas abroad,
  And built the lofty skies.

I sing the wisdom that ordained
  The sun to rule by day;
The moon shines full at his command,
  And all the stars obey.

I sing the goodness of the Lord
  That filled the earth with food;
He formed the creatures with his word,
  And then pronounced them good.

Lord, how Thy wonders are displayed
  Where'er I turn mine eye!
If I survey the ground I tread,
  Or gaze upon the sky!

There's not a flower or plant below,
  But makes Thy glories known;
And clouds arise and tempests blow,
  By order from Thy throne.

Creatures (as numerous as they be)
  Are subject to thy care;
There's not a place where we can flee,
  But God is present there.

In heaven he shines with beams of love,
  With wrath in Hell beneath!
'Tis on the earth I stand or move,
  And 'tis His air I breathe.

His hand is my perpetual guard;
  He keeps me with his eye;
Why should I then forget the Lord,
  Who is for ever nigh?

There, in eight clear, rhythmical, musical quatrains, you have the essence of what has come to be known as the Puritan ethic, but I suspect that most of it could be said or sung just as enthusiastically by an Episcopalian, Catholic, Jewish, or Hindu child. It is the eternal song of man reaching for God. It is at once simple and profound, the ultimate in poetic expression. And who can dispute Watts that a child who has repeated each of these lines over and over again before father and mother in the evening, and again before a school class in the morning, knows it so thoroughly that it is never forgotten? Or consider Divine Song Number Twenty, "Against Idleness and Mischief":

How doth the little busy bee
  Improve each shining hour,
And gather honey all the day
  From every opening flower.

How skillfully she builds her cell!
  How neat she spreads the wax!
And labors hard to store it well
  With the sweet food she makes.

In works of labor or of skill,
  I would be busy too;
For Satan finds some mischief still
  For idle hands to do.

In books, or work, or healthful play,
  Let my first years be past,
That I may give for every day
  A good account at last.

Having concluded his divine songs, Watts then presents a few "Specimens" of moral songs, "in the hope that some happy and condescending genius would undertake to perform much better." The first of these he called "The Sluggard":

'Tis the voice of the sluggard; I just heard him complain,
"You have waked me too soon, I must slumber again."
As the door on its hinges, so he on his bed,
Turns his sides and his shoulders and his heavy head.

"A little more sleep, and a little more slumber;"
Thus he wastes half his days, and his hours without number;
And when he gets up he sits folding his hands,
Or walks about sauntering, or trifling he stands.

I passed by his garden, and saw the wild brier,
The thorn and the thistle grow broader and higher;
The clothes that hang on him are turning to rags;
And his money still wastes, till he starves or he begs.

I made him a visit, still hoping to find
He had took better care for improving his mind.
He told me his dreams, talked of eating and drinking,
But he scarce reads his Bible, and never loves thinking.

Said I then to my heart, "Here's a lesson for me,"
That man's but a picture of what I might be;
But thanks to my friends for their care in my breeding,
Who taught me betimes to love writing and reading.

The influence of this preacher-poet is not to be underestimated by those who would study the social history of the nineteenth century. It surpasses that of the great philosophers in an era that produced both Adam Smith and De Tocqueville.

What would the nineteenth-century leader who graduated from one of those classrooms—say, a Disraeli, a Macaulay, A Gladstone, a Jefferson, a Lincoln, an Emerson—have thought of a society that would tax the busy bee so as to maintain the sluggard in idleness and mischief? Where, he might ask, has wisdom gone? And if we listen carefully, we can hear echo answering: "Gone with poetry!"

I do not mean to imply that Watts was the only poet who wrote directly for early nineteenth-century children. Many responded to his challenge to "perform better," notably Ann and Jane Taylor, who between 1804 and 1810 produced three books, *Original Poems for Infant Minds*, *Hymns for Infant Minds*, and *Rhymes for the Nursery*, which like Watts's own book, went into countless editions in the next fifty years. Then in 1807, William Roscoe, a prosperous Liverpool merchant, went to press with the poem he had written to teach natural history to his own children, *The Butterfly's Ball and the Grasshopper's Feast*, which spawned a host of imitations. The peacock gave an "at home," the lion a rout, the fishes a gala, and so on ad infinitum—all designed to open up the world of nature to the inquiring minds of children. These had nothing to do with either piety or morality but, like the poetry of Watts and the Taylors, were to be committed to memory, repeated in the quiet corners of the home, and declaimed with gestures in the classroom.

But the poetry of Roscoe, Watts and the Taylors was for the younger children, the girls in their first petticoats and the boys just "going into breeches," as Mary Lamb expressed it in the book in which she and her

brother Charles attempted less successfully to improve on Watts's moral
songs. No sooner had they mastered Watts than the children were
handed nice new copies of Lucy Aikin's *Poetry for Children*, consisting of
200 short pieces to be committed to memory, first published in London
in 1802, revised in 1804, and shortly after pirated in America.

Lucy Aikin was well equipped to make judicious selections from the
great poets, for she was the daughter of John Aikin, M.D., and the niece of
his sister, Mrs. Barbauld, both well known to all students of children's
literature. Her short pieces, sometimes ten lines, sometimes fifty, came
from the best work of Shakespeare, Milton, Dryden, Gay, Thomson,
Addison, Young, Goldsmith, Gray, and others who had been immortalized in Samuel Johnson's *Lives of the Poets*. The young scholars, having
now entered what we would call third grade, are asked to memorize such
poetic extracts as this:

> Let wealth, let fame, those dazzling gifts of fate,
> Bless all the wayward sons of pomp or state.
> Be mine the riches of a soul refined,
> The heart benevolent, the spotless mind,
> To heaven's unerring will, to humble hope, resigned.

Or, if the teacher's taste ran to cautionary verses, she might assign this
one:

> The fly about the candle gay dances with thoughtless hum,
> But short, alas, the giddy play, his pleasure proves his doom.
> The child in such simplicity about the beehive clings,
> And with one drop of honey he received a thousand stings.

Or, if the teacher is of a revolutionary turn of mind, she might select this:

> The glories of our birth and state are shadows, not substantial things.
> There is no armor against fate. Death lays his icy hand on kings.
> Sceptre and crown must tumble down, and in the dust be equal made
> With the poor crooked scythe and spade. All must come to the cold tomb.
> Only the actions of the just shall swell and blossom in the dust.

It may seem to the emancipated teacher of our time that there is an
excess of piety and virtue in the classroom poetry of 1820, but that was
the temper of the times. And we cannot overlook the fact that these
poetry-reciting children grew up to be the Tennysons, the Brontes, the
Brownings, the Longfellows, the Poes and the Holmeses who gave us the
glorious age that blossomed in the second half of the nineteenth century.

While the children were under the rigid discipline of Watts and the
Taylors, their parents were enjoying the liberating influence of the
romantic period in the poetry of Wordsworth, Keats, Shelley, Coleridge,
and Byron. Scott's revival of the old ballads, and the enormous popularity

of his own narrative poems, notably "Marmion" and "The Lady of the Lake," created a new interest in romance and adventure. Lockhart had translated the ancient Spanish ballads as early as 1823, and the 1840s saw the publication of Macaulay's *Lays of Ancient Rome*, including "Horatius at the Bridge." Barham had invented the Ingoldsby legends, and Aytoun the Bon Gaultier ballads. Although written for adults, these rollicking rhymes caught the fancy of the children, and it was inevitable that these imaginative tales would lead to similar works written especially for them.

Lewis Carroll (though as Charles Lutwidge Dodgson a lay reader in the Church of England) responded with the two *Alice* books, and was bold enought to include parodies of both Watts and Jane Taylor. The voice of the sluggard became the voice of the lobster, and "Twinkle, twinkle, little star" became "Twinkle, twinkle, little bat." Martin Gardner and I have had great fun trying to identify the real author of "Speak Gently to the Little Child," which Carroll changed to "Speak Roughly to Your Little Boy." George MacDonald, a Scottish preacher-poet turned novelist, gave us *At the Back of the North Wind* and *The Princess and Curdie*. Edward Lear, already famous for his book *Book of Nonsense*, met the demands of the children and of his publishers with "The Owl and the Pussycat" and "The Pobble Who Has No Toes." William S. Gilbert, Judge Edward Parry and others joined the trend toward fantasy, which from that time to the end of the century shared equally with piety and morality in the rich poetic repast spread before the fortunate children.

The years 1870 to 1920 saw the emergence of a host of magazines that were at once popular with the children and commercially successful. Not only were they filled with poetry of a high order, but in many cases the editors were poets themselves, as in the case of Nathaniel Willis of *Youth's Companion* and Mary Mapes Dodge of *St. Nicholas*.

The school readers also maintained the tradition of the early century, and relied heavily on the poets. McGuffey's first eclectic reader and a slate framed with wood were the standard equipment of the six-year-old on the way to school. Once at school, pupils applied themselves to Lesson 56 by writing on the slate:

> God made the little birds to sing
>   And flit from tree to tree
> 'Tis He who sends them in the spring
>   To sing to you and me.

McGuffey's second reader had eighteen poems; the third, thirty; the fourth, thirty-six; the fifth, sixty-one; and the sixth, sixty-two. All the great poets living and dead were represented, and poetry was used to teach reading, writing, spelling, elocution, history, geography, and every other subject in the curriculum. By the time they left school, poetry had become, for all but the dullest of them, part of their lives, and some became accomplished poets, finding a ready outlet for their talent in the local newspapers and the national magazines. When I was a young man in the 1920s, every city of size had a half-dozen dailies, and each had its local poet, many of them conducting special columns. When did you last see a poem in your daily paper?

It came to me as a shock, therefore, when my children went to school in the early thirties, to find that poetry had no place in the curriculum. There were two reasons for this.

My generation had come out of World War I in a spirit of revolt, determined to shake off the old traditions that they considered the main cause of the holocaust which only the luckiest of us had survived. In defiance of the old forms, the poets among us sought a new poetic langauge, and came up with a kind of unstructured verse that sounded more like muddled prose to our elders, accustomed as they were to the orderly metrics and verbal harmonies of the past. Whatever might be said for this new poetry, it could not very well be read to children. I have sometimes thought of experimenting by reading Eliot, Pound and Amy Lowell to a fifth-grade class, but have flinched as the time approached. If some of you have tried it, or would like to try it, I would be happy to hear what luck you have.

A second reason for the eclipse of poetry in the schools was another upsurge of the cultural revolt known as progressive education, which held that repetition of memorized phrases, especially if repeated in unison, stultified the minds of the children and retarded their freedom of expression. The memorization and declamation of peotry, which had been fundamental in the learning process for at least ten generations, was expunged from the classroom. In due course, poetry also disappeared from the public prints, and retreated to the safe heaven of academe, where the art that had been the elixir, the delight and the inspiration of the common people became the resource material of scholarly analysis and interpretation.

A strange paradox in this poetic blight that has come upon us is that we actually have a surprising number of excellent poets, in both Britain and America, writing for children as well as adults. The difficulty is that the channels for reaching both adults and children are not as open to poetry as they were in the days of my youth. Even so excellent a program as "Anyone for Tennyson?" seems no longer able to survive on the public broadcasting network, and we could hardly expect the commercial networks to launch such a program in competition with the violence of "Starsky and Hutch" or the overdramatized news of "60 Minutes."

I hesitate to name any of these fine modern poets, for I would surely miss one who is a favorite with more than one person in this sophisticated audience. I will mention just one, recently gone, unfortunately, to join her peers on the slopes of Parnassus. Phyllis McGinley in 1953 wrote "In Praise of Diversity," a poem which, had it been written in 1853, would have been quoted in every journal and children's reader and made her name immortal. As it was, her passing a year ago went almost unnoticed, and her great philosophic gem has been overlooked by the anthologies and is all but forgotten. The poem consists of fourteen six-line stanzas and is too long to reproduce here. A few of the stanzas should, however, remind you of the poem and will perhaps induce you to read it again:

> One whimsical beatitude
>   Concocted for his gain and glory,
> Has man most stoutly misconstrued
>   Of all the primal category,
> Counting no blessing, but a flaw
> That difference is the mortal law.
> One shrill, monotonous, level note
>   The human orchestra's reduced to.
> Man marks his ballot, turns his coat,
>   Gets born, gets buried, as he used to.
> Makes war, makes love, but with a kind
> Of masked and universal mind.
> Or so it seems. Yet who would dare
>   Deny that nature planned it other,
> When every freckled thrush can wear
>   A dapple different from his brother,
> When each pale snowflake in the storm
> Is false to some imagined norm.
> Rejoice that under cloud and star
>   The planet's more than Maine or Texas.
> Bless the delightful fact there are
>   Twelve months, nine muses, and two sexes;
> And infinite in earth's dominions
> Arts, climates, wonders, and opinions.

The tragedy is that the case of Phyllis McGinley is not an exceptional one. The channels of communication, infinitely superior to those of the 1850s, are to all intents and purposes closed to poetry.

I accepted the invitation to join in this symposium fully aware that you would probably disagree with some of the things I might say. But with my concluding remark I hope there will be unanimous agreement.

As surely as my own generation displaced poetry from its proper place as the mother of the arts, it is the responsibility of your generation to replace it. In language that Isaac Watts might have used, I wish you God-speed!

Z—ZÉNOBIE SAIT COMPTER D'UN JUSQU'À ZÉRO.

John Mackay Shaw, donor and curator of the "Childhood in Poetry" collection now in the library of Florida State University.

CONTRIBUTORS

WALTER L. ARNSTEIN, Professor, University of Illinois.

GILLIAN AVERY, author, Oxford, England.

HARRIETT R. CHRISTY, Owen Ayres & Associates, Eau Claire, Wisconsin.

MARGARET N. COUGHLAN, Children's Literature Center, Library of Congress.

CAROL DOLL, doctoral student, University of Illinois.

CAROLYN L. KARCHER, doctoral student, University of Maryland.

PHYLLIS BIXLER, Assistant Professor, Kansas State University.

SELMA K. RICHARDSON, Associate Professor, University of Illinois.

JOHN MACKAY SHAW, Collector and Bibliographer, Florida State University.

NOTE

Illustrations of the letters of the alphabet in this volume appeared originally in *St. Nicholas,* October 1878.